teach yourself

modern china
michael lynch

For over 60 years, more than
50 million people have learnt over
750 subjects the **teach yourself**
way, with impressive results.

be where you want to be
with **teach yourself**

For UK order enquiries: please contact Bookpoint Ltd, 130 Milton Park, Abingdon, Oxon, OX14 4SB. Telephone: +44 (0) 1235 827720. Fax: +44 (0) 1235 400454. Lines are open 09.00–17.00, Monday to Saturday, with a 24-hour message answering service. Details about our titles and how to order are available at www.teachyourself.co.uk

For USA order enquiries: please contact McGraw-Hill Customer Services, PO Box 545, Blacklick, OH 43004-0545, USA. Telephone: 1-800-722-4726. Fax: 1-614-755-5645.

For Canada order enquiries: please contact McGraw-Hill Ryerson Ltd, 300 Water St, Whitby, Ontario, L1N 9B6, Canada. Telephone: 905 430 5000. Fax: 905 430 5020.

Long renowned as the authoritative source for self-guided learning – with more than 50 million copies sold worldwide – the **teach yourself** series includes over 500 titles in the fields of languages, crafts, hobbies, business, computing and education.

British Library Cataloguing in Publication Data: a catalogue record for this title is available from the British Library.

Library of Congress Catalog Card Number: on file.

First published in UK 2006 by Hodder Education, 338 Euston Road, London, NW1 3BH.

First published in US 2006 by The McGraw-Hill Companies, Inc.

This edition published 2006.

The **teach yourself** name is a registered trade mark of Hodder Headline.

Typeset by Transet Limited, Coventry, England.
Printed in Great Britain for Hodder Education, a division of Hodder Headline, 338 Euston Road, London, NW1 3BH, by Cox & Wyman Ltd, Reading, Berkshire.

The publisher has used its best endeavours to ensure that the URLs for external websites referred to in this book are correct and active at the time of going to press. However, the publisher and the author have no responsibility for the websites and can make no guarantee that a site will remain live or that the content will remain relevant, decent or appropriate.

Hodder Headline's policy is to use papers that are natural, renewable and recyclable products and made from wood grown in sustainable forests. The logging and manufacturing processes are expected to conform to the environmental regulations of the country of origin.

Impression number   10 9 8 7 6 5 4 3 2 1
Year   2010 2009 2008 2007 2006

contents

dedication
for Charlotte Pack

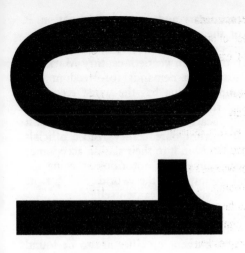

01

China – old and new

This chapter will cover:
- the strange character of modern China
- the China of the emperors
- Confucianism
- the place of violence in modern China.

Modern China is an extraordinary and contradictory nation. It is likely, in the course of the present century, to become the world's strongest economic power. Yet it is ruled by a reactionary socialist oligarchy, a relic of failed twentieth-century Marxism, which refuses to give ground to demands for freedom and democracy. Of all the nations, China has the worst record of human rights' violations. It runs the largest prison camp system on earth, where it annually incarcerates millions of dissidents. It is administered by a vast corrupt bureaucracy whose officials owe their privileged position within it to their slavish acceptance of the official Communist regime. It is notorious as being the most physically polluted country in the world and for its unwillingness to take genuine steps to cleanse itself.

Within its borders are some of the most prosperous regions in the world and some of the poorest. It is both a first world nation and a third world country. In its burgeoning cities are to be found wealthy, ambitious and upwardly mobile young people dwelling in luxury apartments; in its rural areas there are peasants living in dire poverty in mud-walled huts. It has a culture of unmatched antiquity and richness, but modern Chinese draw little inspiration from this, save as a source of tourist income. China's concern is not with the past but the future. In schools and colleges China's young are urged to look forward not back. The past cannot be changed but the future can be constructed. Yet, and this is one of the main themes of this book, there are aspects of present Chinese thinking and attitudes that are explicable only by reference to their historical origins.

Communist rule in China

In September 2005, stewards at the British Labour Party Conference forcibly ejected an 82-year-old man from the hall for shouting 'Nonsense!' during a speech from the platform by the Foreign Secretary of the day, Jack Straw. Thankfully, none of the stewards was injured. In May 2006, in the dead of night, 76 Metropolitan police officers in a meticulously planned raid, which had been ordered by the Home Office, tore down the banners erected by a lone anti-war protester outside Parliament and arrested him. Thankfully, none of the policemen was injured.

These were acts that won the hearty approval of the Communist government of the People's Republic of China (PRC). How dare one individual insult a member of the ruling Party! How dare one man think he knew better than the government!

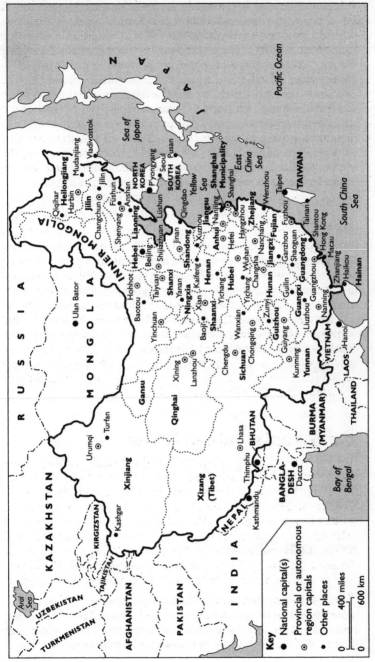

figure 1 modern China

A regretful Labour Party and its leader subsequently apologized for the first action and admitted in embarrassment that the second had been an overreaction. That is where they lost the support of the PRC. The retraction was incomprehensible to the Chinese government, which was similarly baffled by the climb-down of the French government in 2006 when it abandoned its education reforms in the face of student protests. The PRC showed the same attitude in Africa where, keen to spread its commercial interests, it was full of praise for Robert Mugabe's dictatorship in Zimbabwe. In the theory and practice of the Chinese Communist Party (CCP) which runs China, it is the role of the government to rule; it is the duty of the citizen to obey. In modern China the collective will of the people, as expressed in the CCP, must not be challenged by a mere individual or set of individuals. So, why should a government apologize for doing its duty?

How rigidly the communist rulers of China held to that belief had been graphically shown in an incident in June 1989 that shocked the world – the violent suppression of a demonstration in Tiananmen Square in Beijing when guns and tanks were used to disperse a student protest. It is the argument of this book that the ferocity with which the government treats dissent and opposition is a defining characteristic of the Chinese nation. Modern China is a product of violence.

The rule of the CCP in China dates back to 1949. However, the principle on which its power rests, the absolute right of the central authority to govern, goes back 4,000 years. The near half-century of communist dictatorship is a mere addendum to millennia of rule by the Chinese emperors. This book sets out to describe and explain the structure of modern China; it does so by putting China in its historical context. Of course, all nations and all peoples are a product of their history. But there is a special sense in which China is a reflection of its past, in a way which no other nation is.

Imperial China

Until the early nineteenth century China had regarded itself as a society supreme over all others. It had occasional contacts with the outside world, but it never considered these as especially significant. It retained a sense of its own uniqueness. Under the rule of its emperors, who had exercised absolute authority for thousands of years, it had developed a deep belief that it was a self-sufficient culture which needed nothing from foreign nations. The dismissive Chinese term to describe the people of other nations was 'barbarians'. One crucial consequence of this Sino-centric view of themselves was that the Chinese were slow to develop a concept of progress. Why change when we have all we need? China's rulers saw no necessity to introduce reform. This derived not from idleness or lack of imagination but from adherence to certain patterns of thought – Taoism and Confucianism – that had dominated Chinese culture since the fifth century BC.

Taoism and Confucianism

Many key Chinese words do not have an exact counterpart in English. 'Taoism' is one of these. Subtleties are often lost in translation. Nonetheless, a workable definition can be offered. The basic notion in Taoism is that there is a fundamental force, the 'tao', which holds existence together and provides the harmony of nature. The historical importance of this idea is that it was adopted by a highly influential Chinese thinker known in the West by his Latinized name, Confucius, who incorporated it into his philosophy. Confucius was not a mere player with ideas and words; his approach was very practical. Confucianism is sometimes loosely defined as a religion, but this gives the wrong picture. Confucius (551–479BC) was not a religious thinker in Western terms. He did not concern himself with the concept of a God or gods, not because he denied their existence, but because, if they did exist, they were unknowable. His preoccupation was with the knowable world. Confucius started from what for him were four fundamental and self-evident truths:

- Individuals are born into an existing world in which other people also live.
- It is the responsibility of each individual to accept the real world as he finds it and to relate harmoniously to the people in it.
- Social harmony is essential to individual happiness.
- Social harmony is possible only if each individual lives an ordered life.

But how were individuals to know how to live an ordered life and so preserve harmony? The answer was provided by Confucius and a later disciple of his, Mencius. They constructed a code of social conduct based on their observation of how human beings acted and reacted in their relations with each other. The code was the guide to right behaviour. The character of the guide can be glimpsed in the following quotations from what are known as 'the analects of Confucius', the collected sayings of the master.

'What you do not wish for yourself, do not do to others.'

'Since you yourself desire status, then help others achieve it. Since you yourself desire success, then help others attain it.'

'Look at nothing in defiance of ritual, listen to nothing in defiance of ritual, speak of nothing in defiance of ritual, never stir hand or foot in defiance of ritual.'

What the first two sayings illustrate is the need to put others before self. Self-restraint is the basis of the well-lived life; selfishness is the destroyer of social harmony. The third quotation points to the great weight Confucius laid on formal ceremony; how neighbour greeted neighbour, how a child acknowledged a parent, how an official honoured the emperor. For Confucius, ritual and the rules of etiquette that accompanied it were not ends in themselves; they were the mechanisms by which the individual exercised self-restraint, showed respect for others, and contributed to an orderly, structured society.

There is no doubt that at its best Confucianism recognized individual worth and promoted social well-being. Confucius himself said that the humblest peasant was as capable of virtue and, therefore, as deserving of respect as the highest official. But there was always a danger that the subtleties of Confucianism would be ignored and it would simply become a system for maintaining the status quo and preventing change. For much of Chinese history this is what happened. Too often Confucian principles deteriorated into a series of do's and don'ts imposed by the stronger upon the weaker. For example, one of the most powerful of the Confucian teachings was that society rested on the *san gang*, the three essential bonds. These were the respect of children for their parents, the obedience of wives to their husbands, and the loyalty of people to the emperor. It is easy to see how these bonds could become distorted into a form of dominance, exploitation and tyranny. Confucianism became a charter for those in authority.

The stress in Confucianism on the duty of the individual to preserve social harmony by accepting things as he found them and by conforming to existing laws and conventions was a very effective political tool for those in power. It is obvious why Confucianism appealed to China's successive emperors. The absolute right of the emperor to rule had been established by force of arms. What was needed was a justification for holding power that did not depend solely on military might. Confucianism provided exactly that by stressing that obedience to proper authority was essential to the existence of a virtuous, harmonious society. Emperors consistently claimed that anyone who disputed their control was damaging the proper and natural order of things and was not to be tolerated. Such challengers became social outcasts and were treated with great severity. China gained a reputation for the merciless way it dealt with internal rebels.

Yet rebels were sometimes successful and took power for themselves. How was this to be explained in Confucian terms? Had not the rebels broken the rules of harmony? Not according to 'the mandate of heaven'. This was a neat piece of logic that explained how change could occur in an unchanging system and at the same time be in keeping with Confucian principles. If an emperor behaved without virtue and oppressed his people unfairly, then he had broken the rules of harmony and thereby sacrificed his claim to the obedience of his subjects. He had forfeited the mandate of heaven, his right to govern. 'Heaven' in this context did not mean the home of the gods; like the tao, it referred to the force that kept things in proper balance. What the new emperor had done by overthrowing his tyrannical predecessor was to restore the harmony that had been disturbed. This was the argument that justified successful rebellion. It was a form of justification by success and it left a lasting mark on Chinese politics. Things had to work to be respected. Few Chinese were moved by appeals to tradition. Political failure was seldom forgiven.

Providing as it did the justification for the political establishment to maintain itself in power, Confucianism came to pervade public life in China. Its key precepts of placing the good of society before the rights of the individual and of obeying legitimate authority continue to this day to colour Chinese thinking. A key group to benefit from Confucianism in imperial China were the mandarins. These were an élite body of scholars who formed the civil service in China. The mandarins went through a series of rigid examinations in Confucian thought. Once they had passed these, they joined an exclusive class of officials who ran China under the authority of the emperor. The mandarins did not survive long into the twentieth century but their existence over thousands of years left a tradition of bureaucratic control by an exclusive group of privileged officials that is exactly paralleled by the rule of the Communist Party in modern China.

Buddhism

In reality the Confucian pattern of civil obedience often broke down. Famines were frequent in China and at such times public order was difficult to maintain. Much of Chinese history was the story of a recurrent struggle between the imperial authorities and starving peasants. The Taiping Rebellion in the middle years of the nineteenth century was the most vivid example of a peasant rising. Nevertheless, Confucianism provided the underpinning of Chinese society. It offered an ideal of social behaviour even though the ideal was not always observed. In that respect it might be compared to the way in which Christianity provided the basic values in European society. One interesting feature of Confucianism was that, since in strict terms it was not a religion, it was accommodating to other faiths. That is why it proved perfectly compatible with Buddhism, the other great influence on traditional Chinese thought. Buddhism, which originated in India around the same time as Confucianism in China, is a faith which teaches its members to seek personal enlightenment by a series of increasingly difficult spiritual exercises. Its contemplative nature and encouragement of the individual to control his appetites and cravings, ensured that Buddhism appealed to the same values that inspired Confucianism. Many Chinese were happily Taoist, Confucian and Buddhist all at the same time. They saw no contradiction between the different philosophies.

The shattering of imperial China's isolation

As political conservatives, the mandarins had a vested interest in perpetuating the concept of China as a nation whose unchanging, permanent character was the proof of its unique worth. *Zhongguo* is the Chinese word for China; it means 'the centre of the earth', a clear indication of China's view that it was a superior nation. In the days of the emperors, Chinese map-makers always put China in the centre with the rest of the world circling round it.

But, while China might have regarded itself as special, other parts of the world did not. By the nineteenth century the major trading nations in Europe were searching for new markets and resources in Asia. China became a target. To the profound dismay of the Chinese they found they were not strong enough to resist European demands. China was obliged to open its ports to foreign traders and to sign a set of what became known as 'unequal treaties' under which it gave over territory and accepted trade on very disadvantageous terms. One of the most notorious examples of such humiliation was China's defeat at the hands of the British in the opium wars of the mid-nineteenth century. In the early 1840s, Britain issued an ultimatum to China: it was told to increase its imports of opium from British India or face attack. When the Chinese were slow to respond, Britain carried out her threat by sending gunboats to blast Canton into submission. Much the same story was repeated in the 1850s when another British bombardment was launched. The consequence was that a defeated China had to accept a huge increase in the import of a drug that debilitated many of its people and to hand over territory, including Hong Kong, to British control. Where Britain had led, other western nations were quick to follow. By 1900 over 50 Chinese 'treaty ports' were in British, German, French or Portugese hands. China's island neighbour, Japan, also got in on the act, winning a war against China in 1895 and seizing Chinese land.

Coinciding with the opium wars was an event which in domestic terms was as damaging to the imperial system and to China's special sense of its own worth as was its subjection to foreign demands. Between 1850 and 1864 there occurred possibly the most destructive internal rebellion in world history. It was a peasant rising against the imperial government of the Qing, the royal dynasty that had ruled China since 1644. Peasant risings had been frequent throughout Chinese history. Invariably, these had been local affairs, which were crushed with ease and were followed by the rebel leaders' summary execution for daring to challenge the divine rule of the emperors. The Taiping Rebellion that began in 1850 was different; it lasted 15 years, affected large areas of China, and was eventually put down only with the greatest difficulty. Approximately 30 million died before the Rebellion was finally crushed.

From Revolution to Revolution, 1911–49

In 1911 China underwent the first of its modern revolutions when the Qing dynasty collapsed. The truth was the Qing had been tottering for decades and the only surprise was that they lasted as long as they did. In 1900, in a movement known as the Boxer rising, they had led a challenge to foreign domination, but it was a desperate affair and was crushed with great brutality by an international force raised from the armies of the various powers in China. The Chinese were forced to watch as mass beheadings took place. The Qing survived but their credibility had gone. Eleven years later the long-awaited Chinese Revolution duly occurred; when faced by mutinous troops they could not control the Qing decided to abdicate rather than wait to be overthrown by force.

The imperial system was replaced by a republic which claimed authority over the whole of China but which in reality lacked real power. For the next four decades, the period of 'the warlords', conflicting groups and interests struggled to impose themselves on China. The general hatred of the warlords and of the continuing subjection of China to foreign influence, expressed itself in a driving desire for Chinese regeneration known as the May Fourth Movement. On that date in 1919, there was an outburst of anger in Beijing when the news came through that the peace treaty makers at Versailles had decided that the Chinese territories that Germany had formerly occupied would not be returned to China; instead they were to be given to Japan. Taking advantage of the national outrage this created, two main revolutionary parties gathered strength. One was the Nationalists or Guomindang (GMD) created by Sun Yatsen and led after 1925 by Chiang Kaishek; the other was the Chinese Communist Party (CCP), whose leader from the later 1920s was Mao Zedong.

At first the two parties co-operated but then turned on each other in a vicious civil war that lasted intermittently until 1949. Although the Nationalists formed the internationally recognized government of China from the early 1930s, they proved incapable of destroying their Communist rivals. The final outcome was the complete victory of Mao's Communist forces. In 1949 Chiang's Nationalists were driven from China to their one remaining haven, the island of Taiwan, leaving Mao free to declare formally that the Communist revolution had succeeded and that the mainland was now the People's Republic of China.

The Japanese occupation, 1931–45

In a sense the bitter episodes listed above were largely self-inflicted. They arose out of Chinese responses to Chinese problems. But in this period China also underwent a searing humiliation imposed from outside – occupation by Japan. This proved another of modern China's violently formative experiences. In 1931, Japanese forces began an occupation of China that was to last until 1945 and make China a major theatre of the Second World War. The invasion of China was part of Japan's bid for supremacy in Asia. There was the deeply held belief among the Japanese that they were a superior race, supreme among Asian peoples. It was the eastern equivalent of the Nazi belief that the Germanic people were a master race. This concept of racial superiority had the most appalling consequences for the Chinese. Sakai Ryu, one of the commanders of the first invasion force to arrive in northern China in 1937, remarked, 'The Chinese people are bacteria infesting world civilization'. His racism helps to explain the bestiality with which the Japanese treated the Chinese during the occupation. It was tied in with the Japanese equivalent of lebensraum (living space) – the idea that, because Japan was becoming overpopulated and was fast running out of resources, it had every right to expand into other areas of Asia in order to guarantee its survival and continuation as a great nation. It followed that those who resisted its rightful march deserved no mercy. Speaking to a foreign reporter, Lieutenant Ryukichi of the imperial Japanese Army remarked, 'You and I have diametrically different views of the Chinese. You may be dealing with them as human beings, but I regard them as swine. We can do anything to such creatures.'

It was such attitudes that created the frenzied blood-lust that resulted in arguably one of the worst atrocities in twentieth-century warfare – the rape of Nanjing. In December 1937, Japanese troops broke into the fortified city and proceeded to carry out the specific order of their commander, Asaka Yasuhiko, to 'Kill all Captives'. Over the course of four weeks 300,000 Chinese people were murdered in a variety of ways: these including shooting by pistol, rifle or machine gun, beheading, burying alive, bayoneting, drenching in kerosene or petrol and setting on fire, and suspending on meat hooks. Around 20,000 women were rounded up and gang raped regardless of their age or fragility. Many were so abused that they died from the rape itself or the mutilations that were inflicted afterwards; those who did not were bayoneted to death. A Japanese private later confessed, 'We sent out coal trucks to the city streets and villages to seize a lot of women. And then each of them was allocated to 15 to 20 soldiers for sexual intercourse and abuse.' To this day there has not been a full acknowledgement by Japan of the scale of its wartime atrocities. China's anger was recently raised when it was realized that Japanese school books either omit any reference to the horrors or gloss over them in such a way that their true character is hidden. There was also much Chinese bitterness when, in 1978, Japan built the Yasukini shrine, a monument honouring the nation's wartime dead, which included the names of 14 soldiers who had been convicted as war criminals in the trials held by the Allies after the war. China is offended by the readiness of some Japanese opinion makers to portray their country's wartime record as heroic and honourable. From time to time, China has raised the issue of compensation with its neighbour, asking that recompense be made to the surviving victims and to the families blighted by the murders and atrocities in which the Japanese troops indulged. In the early years of the present century large groups of little old ladies were frequently to be seen in China's main cities demanding redress for great wrongs done to them 60 years earlier. These were the 'comfort women', the euphemism for those Chinese girls who had been seized during the war and forced to work in the brothels specially set up for the troops of the Japanese army.

The character of modern Chinese history

Savagery within and humiliation from without had been the main features of nineteenth-century China. The twentieth century was to be even more violent. Modern China was forged in the crucible of bitter domestic turmoil, brutal foreign occupation, destructive civil war and deadly political strife. It was to be denied the possibility of ordered progression and peaceful adjustment. A constant reversion to violent upheaval was to disfigure China's development in the twentieth century.

Modern China, therefore, is the product of a series of dramatic and violent crises. There was nothing evolutionary about its development in the twentieth century. It was wrenched into modernity. To understand the character of modern China we have to understand the major upheavals through which it passed. These may be listed as the Revolution of 1911–12 that saw the end of imperial rule, the running civil war between revolutionary factions that tore China apart, and the savage Japanese invasion and occupation of China between 1937 and 1945. The traumas were to continue in the second half of the century. They took their bitterest form in the terrible famine that accompanied Mao Zedong's Great Leap Forward, the horrors of the Cultural Revolution, and the tragedies of the new era when Deng Xiaoping tried to modernize China economically while continuing to suppress it politically. An analysis of these great formative experiences that the Chinese people underwent will help to explain how modern China came to be the nation it is.

What the history of the twentieth century makes clear is that China simply did not have the social or political traditions to allow it to make a smooth transition from its conservative Confucian past to modernity. Things changed in a series of savage lurches. Violence ruled; it was the only means by which power could be achieved. Those who wanted to hold authority could do so only by obliterating their opponents. It is a pattern that is still observable in China today.

02

Mao Zedong – creator or destroyer?

This chapter will cover:

- Mao's impact on China
- Mao's career
- Mao's legacy
- Mao's reputation
- Mao's image.

Mao's place in modern Chinese history

A century ago China had been written off by the advanced world. The common view was that it was so backward it could never become a truly modern state. Large parts of its territory were occupied by European powers and it was subject to their laws. China was a plaything of the Western world. Yet in the lifetime of Mao Zedong (1893–1976), China rose to be a great nation. It threw off its shackles and regained its independence. It was Mao who made it happen. When, in the 1960s, thousands of ecstatic young Chinese chanted his name, waved his little red book, and cried 'Chairman Mao, may you live for a thousand years', they were saluting him as the supreme hero who had freed their country from a century of humiliation at the hands of the foreigner. In their eyes, Mao Zedong was the god-like figure who had led a vast social revolution and had made China a great world power, possessing its own nuclear weapons and bidding to displace the Soviet Union as the leader of international socialism.

These were momentous successes. But they came at a terrible price. The more we learn about Mao, the more we realize how lethally ruthless he was. In attempting to reshape China in his own image he caused the death of 70 million Chinese, a scale of destruction unmatched in world history. It was a fearful legacy to leave his people.

Mao's early years

Mao was born in 1893 into a peasant family in Shaoshan, a village in the Hunan province of southern China. By local standards Mao's family could be counted prosperous. His father had made enough money as a rice trader to branch into money lending. By the time of Mao's birth the family owned some 30 acres and took on hired labourers to help plant and gather the rice. The farmhouse in which Mao was raised was one of the largest dwellings in the area. At the height of Mao's power in the 1960s and 1970s, its mud floor and walls and its thatched roof were renovated and it was turned into a place of pilgrimage to which millions flocked. The pilgrims dropped off in number after Mao's death, but the house still stands as a museum.

Most teenagers in most cultures are obnoxious; Mao certainly was. His later defenders said he was a natural rebel but this may simply be another way of saying he was a selfish brat who would not do what he was told. Rensheng, his father, certainly saw it that way. He could not understand why his son would not show him the proper deference that was the duty of all Chinese children. On one occasion Mao threatened to drown himself in the local pond rather than apologize for having insulted his father's friends and submit to a thrashing. The threat worked and Rensheng withdrew the demand for a public apology and abandoned the beating. Mao had chosen his place of resistance carefully; locals believed the pond was haunted by the spirit of a young girl who had been drowned in it as punishment for refusing to marry the man of her parents' choice. The villagers, including young Mao, had watched while the girl had been strapped head down to a heavy plank and submerged until she drowned. The story is still told by the guides at the local museum as an example of the female oppression that had prevailed in the China of Mao's youth. Certainly, the drowning was one in a series of violent episodes to which Mao was exposed as he grew up.

Such family affection as Mao felt was all directed towards his mother whom he adored. Although, in accordance with rural tradition, she played a subservient role in the household, keeping her peace and obeying her husband, Mao admired her for her generous and forgiving nature. At her death in 1919, he described her as having been like 'the sunshine in spring and the morning clouds'. It never seemed to bother him that she was a devout Buddhist. Later, as leader of Communist China, he was to outlaw all religions as feudal superstitions, yet Mao was too Chinese not to be superstitious himself. Throughout his career he looked for portents and good omens before making his decisions.

Mao's education was a chequered affair. He was very intelligent and very well read. He eventually trained as a teacher but never quite made it to university, except as an assistant librarian in Beijing. He was not an easy pupil or student; if he did not like a subject or a teacher he simply made no effort. But in subjects which interested him and with teachers who inspired him, he worked with a will. The books he first read were the romantic yarns of old China, such as The Water Margin and The Three Kingdoms, tales of action and adventure. But the classics also came to impress him, and, although he found them difficult, their military and political themes became a lifelong interest. Even after he came to power he continued to read them for practical guidance. As a young man, Mao immersed himself in philosophy and politics and came to admire a number of major western writers whose works he read in translation; among these were Charles Darwin and John Stuart Mill. He loved wrestling with intellectual arguments and became convinced that life was dialectical; that is to say, a struggle between opposite forces, only one of which could win. This was as true of human beings as it was of the world of nature. He admired those leaders in history who, having overcome their rivals, imposed order and authority. In his youth Mao was fond of wearing the flowing robes associated with Confucian scholars. That may not have been wholly a coincidence. It is not too fanciful to think that had Mao been born into another time and another place in China he might well have become a Confucian scholar himself, even a mandarin perhaps.

As a teenager, Mao played a minor role as a volunteer soldier in Changsha in the Chinese Revolution of 1911. His experience convinced him that the fall of the Qing had brought China little benefit. Although a republic had replaced the imperial system, the real power lay with the local warlords. Mao recorded the savagery that became commonplace. He described how Changsha was several times overrun by the forces of rival warlords. He listed the brutal punishments he had seen inflicted on the peasants who refused to co-operate with the invading armies: 'gouging out eyes, ripping out tongues, disembowelling and decapitation, slashing with knives and grinding with sand, burning with kerosene and branding with red hot irons'.

The barbarity Mao witnessed greatly affected him. Yet, his reaction was not so much one of horror at the inhumanity as a realization that violence was essential to the gaining and holding of power. No cause could triumph unless it was prepared to use the utmost force. This helps to explain why throughout his career he had no compunction about employing brutal means to crush political opponents. One of his most revealing sayings was, 'all power grows out of the barrel of a gun'.

Mao becomes a Communist

In 1919 Mao moved to Beijing where he became caught up in the excitement of the May Fourth Movement. It was there that he was introduced to Marxist ideas and developed the conviction that if China was to be truly regenerated it would have to undergo a profound social and political revolution. In 1921 Mao became one of the founder members of the Chinese

Communist Party. He played a key role in organizing the alliance between the Nationalists and the Communists that overcame the warlords between 1924 and 1927. However, it was in 1927 that the Nationalist leader, Chiang Kaishek, turned on the Communists and tried to destroy them in the 'White Terror' extermination campaign. Mao managed to survive by taking his CCP forces to the mountains of Jiangxi province, where he began organizing a guerrilla resistance.

Over the next seven years Mao created the Jiangxi Soviet, based on the principle that in China the Communist revolution would be a peasant revolution. His thinking was simple and practical. Since China's industrial workers accounted for less than 4 per cent of the population, whereas the peasants comprised over 80 per cent, if there was to be a popular revolution it would have to be the work of the peasantry.

It was also during the Jiangxi period (1927–34) and his building of a communist 'Red Army' that Mao again revealed the ruthlessness that characterized his whole career. In the notorious 'Futian incident' in 1930 he ordered the torture and execution of some 4,000 Red Army troops whom he accused of plotting against him. His written instruction read: 'Do not kill the important leaders too quickly, but squeeze out of them the maximum information'.

The Long March, 1934–5

By 1934, Chiang Kaishek's Nationalists had surrounded the CCP base in Jiangxi and were close to crushing the Communists completely. But again Mao survived, this time by abandoning Jiangxi and leading the Communists in a desperate flight to Yanan in northern China. The journey to Yanan, which took over a year to complete, was later elevated by CCP propaganda into one of the great epics of Communist folklore – the Long March. It was never as glorious as the propagandists made out; of the 100,000 who fled from Jiangxi, scarcely 20,000 survived to reach their destination. Nevertheless, the March marked a critical stage in Mao's career since it was during the March that he outmanoeuvred his rivals and established himself as leader of the Chinese Communists.

The Yanan Years, 1935–45

The Yanan period was the time when Mao produced the main body of his philosophical and political writings. These were part of his armoury for imposing his personal authority on the CCP. During the Yanan period Mao, with a combination of political skill and unflinching severity, succeeded in gaining complete domination. In 1942 he launched a series of 'rectification of conduct' campaigns; these were a set of purges by means of which he removed his opponents within the party. It was also during this time that Mao developed the strategy begun in Jiangxi of winning over or coercing the peasants into supporting the Communists. His success in this had the double effect of providing military recruits for the anti-Japanese struggle and political supporters for the CCP in its campaign against the urban-based GMD.

Victory over the GMD, 1945–9

With the defeat of Japan at the end of the Second World War in 1945, the CCP turned on the GMD in a renewal of the civil war that had lasted intermittently since the late 1920s. Although Chiang Kaishek's Nationalists had been the official government of China for nearly a decade they had little to show for it. They had become a byword for corruption and, in spite of their greater numbers and the continued support they received from the USA, they had lost the military initiative. A fierce four-year struggle for supremacy ended with the complete victory of the Communists. By 1949 Chiang and the Guomindang had been driven from the Chinese mainland; their one remaining stronghold was the offshore island of Taiwan. Mao and the CCP were now able to begin establishing their Communist rule over the whole of mainland China.

The creation of the People's Republic of China

In Beijing on 1 October 1949, Mao formally declared the People's Republic of China (PRC) to have come into being. He was now in a position to shape China to his own design. His political approach could not have been simpler: China was to be a one-party state and the people were to act in total conformity to the dictates of the new government. It was a system that the emperors of old would have immediately recognized.

The government deliberately created an atmosphere of fear and uncertainty by a series of 'anti-movements', launched against those whom the CCP regarded as socially or politically suspect. The Chinese people were encouraged to expose anyone, friend, neighbour, workmate or even family relation who showed unwillingness to accept the new regime. A whole government department was created to draw up a *dangan*, a dossier, on every suspected Chinese person. The vengeful atmosphere thus created was intensified by Mao's decision to enter the Korean War (1950–53) in support of the North Koreans. This struggle provided further reasons for the government to demand solidarity and loyalty from the people. Landlords were brutally dispossessed of their properties.

Mao's purges extended to the Communist Party itself. Members thought to be less than fully committed to Mao and the new China were branded as 'rightists', opponents of the PRC. A variant on the purges was the periodic invitation to members to criticize government and party policies. This did not denote a softening of the hard line. It was a technique for exposing possible backsliders and opponents. This became very clear in 1957 when Mao, using the slogan 'Let a hundred flowers bloom; let a hundred schools of thought contend', called on members to come into the light and debate the great issues facing China. It was a ruse. Those who were gullible enough to respond as Mao suggested were then arrested as 'rightists'. Such purges were to become a recurrent feature of Chinese politics down to Mao's death in 1976.

The Great Leap Forward, 1958–62

Although Mao had led a great peasant movement to victory in 1949, his aim, nonetheless, was to develop China as an industrial power. He believed that at some time in the near future China would catch up with the Soviet Union and the capitalist West in industrial production. This could be achieved by a huge collective endeavour of the Chinese people. Sheer commitment would make up for their nation's lack of capital and technology. Mao adopted a series of five-year plans modelled on those developed by Stalin in the Soviet Union. These involved prodigious efforts by the Chinese workers. The image of the workers toiling in their millions to fulfil their leader's plans is nicely caught in the description of Mao as 'the emperor of the blue ants'. But impressive though these efforts were, the fact was that Mao had got his economics wrong. His emphasis on heavy industry and mass labour showed how out of date he was. Modern economies are built on hi-tech and special skills, not on will power alone. Good will does not necessarily produce good steel. The shortcomings of Mao's approach were revealed during the five-year plan of 1958–62. Trumpeted by Mao as 'the Great Leap Forward', the plan failed to meet its industrial targets. What was catastrophically worse was the widespread famine that resulted from it.

China's great famine

Between 1959 and 1963 China experienced the greatest famine in human history. During those years perhaps as many as 50 million Chinese died from starvation. It was a catastrophe that the Chinese government refused to acknowledge and Western governments refused to believe. What made the death toll so appalling was not simply its sheer scale but the fact that the tragedy was man-made; it might equally fairly be said to have been Mao-made.

The first step in the Great Leap Forward had been a mass collectivization programme under which the land was taken from the peasants and private ownership ended. Mao ordered that the nation's half a billion peasants were to live and work in communes. There were 70,000 of these created across China. No individual peasants or families would any longer be able to farm for themselves or make a profit. Everything was now to be shared within the local commune. Any surpluses became the property of the state, to be invested in industrial growth.

Mao's belief was that collectivization would lead to a great increase in food production. The opposite happened. Disorientated by the revolution in their way of life, the peasants were unable to adapt quickly to the new system imposed on them. By tradition, most peasants were subsistence farmers, growing just enough food for their families. They did not have the knowledge or the aptitude to farm on a large communal scale. Crop yields fell sharply and hunger became widespread.

Blaming the reported shortfalls on poor local management and the hoarding of grain by rich exploiting peasants, Mao pressed ahead with collectivization. He claimed that it was the peasant masses who were demanding to be collectivized and he was simply heeding their call. It was a lie, of course, but officials who expressed doubts were replaced, while peasants who protested were thrown into camps where they were worked and starved to death. In order not to fall foul of Mao, everybody joined in the lie. Production figures were rigged to show how plentiful the harvests had now become. The party launched a propaganda campaign detailing the benefits of collectivization. Newspapers, newsreels and bill-posters carried images of beaming peasants gathering and storing giant mounds of grain and rice. A large photo that was frequently used depicted children jumping on the top of crops that grew so abundantly in the fields that the children did not fall through. It was announced that so much was being produced that China could now begin to sell the surplus abroad for money to finance its industrial take-off.

Not only was Mao committed to collectivization as the most advanced form of socialist planning, he had also developed what proved to be a lethal belief in 'socialist science'. He had fallen for the notion that there were such things as 'super-crops' that could be grown by following socialist principles. The idea came from the work of Lysenko, a Soviet agronomist who claimed to have produced socialist crops that gave 16 times the yield of the bourgeois variety. Lysenko was a complete fraud and his ideas were blithering nonsense. Nevertheless, Mao fell for them. In 1958, Mao ordered that Lysenkoism was to be strictly followed in the selection and cultivation of China's crops. Chinese experts who were not convinced by the concept of 'socialist science' were to be dismissed. The result was devastation; crops did not multiply, they withered. As with the collectivization disaster, Mao refused to accept he had got it wrong. He attributed the destructive results not to Lysenko's absurd theories but to a failure to apply them properly.

The famine affected all areas of China but it was most severe in the rural provinces of central China. In a great sweep of suffering from Shandong in the east to Tibet in the west millions died from hunger and disease. Of all the forms of death, starvation is among the worst. It destroys body and spirit. The hungry lose the very sense that makes them human. Dignity and restraint die within them long before their bodies finally succumb. As China's famine spread its ravages, parents sold their children, husbands sold their wives, and women sold themselves for food. Peasants offered themselves as slaves to anyone who would feed them. Cannibalism became common. Between 1958 and 1962, millions of Chinese starved to death, the lowest figure has been put at 30 million, the highest at 50 million. By his adherence to collectivization and false science, Mao had turned China's rural provinces into killing fields.

There was no open criticism of Mao over the famine, nor did he acknowledge responsibility for it. Nevertheless, in the early 1960s he withdrew into the political background, leaving two prominent party figures, Deng Xiaoping and Liu Shaoqi, with the task of restoring food supplies. Their attempts to do so led them to abandon collectivization. Mao, however, saw this as an undermining of the socialist principles on which China's Communist revolution rested. In 1966, in a series of dramatic gestures, which included his swimming in the Yangzi, the ageing Chairman reappeared in public and reasserted his dominance in Chinese politics. What prompted him to return was the fear that the revolution he had led was slipping away from him and might not survive his death. In an attempt to leave an indelible mark on China, Mao introduced the Cultural Revolution, a movement that plunged China into a decade of turmoil.

The Cultural Revolution, 1966–76

The Cultural Revolution was such an extraordinary episode and one so central in the development of modern China that a separate chapter in this book has been devoted to it. However, it is important to place it in the context of Mao's leadership of China. Mao's objective in unleashing the Cultural Revolution was to oblige the Party to acknowledge its errors and purge itself of all possible rivals to his authority. It was a means of fulfilling his concept of 'continuing revolution', the belief that unless the Communist Party was regularly purified it would cease to be a revolutionary force and China would cease to be truly socialist. The violence of the movement was not an accidental accompaniment but an essential ingredient.

Mao's legacy

Mao Zedong stands with Lenin, Stalin and Hitler as one of 'the makers of the twentieth century'. Beginning in the 1920s, he created a peasant movement that carried him and his Chinese

Communist Party to power in 1949. It was an extraordinary accomplishment that ranks with the Russian Revolution of 1917. Between the founding of the People's Republic of China in 1949 and Mao's death in 1976, Maoism became the inspiration and hope of a range of anti-colonial movements worldwide and was taken up enthusiastically by many revolutionary hopefuls in the Western world. The subsequent abandonment of Maoism in China and its decline as an inspirational force internationally, does not lessen the magnitude of Mao's achievement in having led to victory the century's largest popular movement.

Unsurprisingly, Mao continues to excite fierce controversy. In the latest major biography of him by Jung Chang (2005), the writer paints him as a monster who cynically exploited the Chinese people for his own corrupt ends. Jung Chang's bitterness is understandable; she had lived under Mao and seen her family destroyed by his policies. But there are grounds for suggesting the lady doth protest too much. Perhaps her closeness to the events distorts her view. Lee Feigon, an American scholar, while acknowledging Mao's bloodstained record, emphasizes the positives. He sees him as the indispensable leader who ended a century and a half of Chinese humiliation and raised his nation to world power status, capable in the twenty-first century of competing on equal terms with all its industrial and commercial competitors.

It could be said, however, that this view is itself a distortion. It is equally arguable that Mao Zedong, rather than carrying China forward, returned it to its blood-soaked past. After all, it was not during Mao's time but only after it that China began to modernize. Whether, as Jung Chang suggests, Mao deliberately intended the horrors that befell China under him is open to debate. What has now been established beyond question is that his policies did cause unprecedented suffering to the Chinese people. There are guilty consciences over this in the Western world. Extraordinary though it now appears, there were many intellectuals in the USA and Europe who in the 1960s and 1970s lauded Mao as a heroic figure, a leader shaping a new brand of humanized communism that might save the world. There are not many left who would argue that now.

Modern China was born in violence and continues to be shaped by it. Mao, its outstanding leader in the twentieth century, was a product of violent times. All the changes that he sought to bring to China were accomplished through violence. Even when his intentions were benign and he genuinely intended to bring the people benefits, he resorted to disruptive means to do so. He knew no other way. The term 'red emperor' fits him perfectly. He ruled by a new form of divine right, not one based on religious or spiritual values, but deriving from the secular concept of historical determinism. History was on his side or, rather, to put it as he saw it, he and the party he led were the instruments of historical change. The China he grew up in had taught him nothing else.

Mao's image

There was a time in the late 1990s when the visitor to China could pick up Mao memorabilia at every street corner. Stall vendors and hawkers were eager to haggle over a great array of items: banners, flags, posters, badges, watches, cigarette lighters, all bearing the Chairman's visage. The flow has dried up somewhat of late, but it is still possible for the determined buyer to purchase Mao souvenirs. The best known image of him is that painted in 1949 by the artist Zhang Zhenshi, showing Mao at the age of 56. It is a magnified copy of this painting that looks out over Tiananmen Square from the wall of the Forbidden City. The image soon became the most popular and easily recognized portrayal in China and in 1962 appeared on the inside cover of the Little Red Book that sold in millions throughout China. Its iconic status was recognized in the West when, around the time of the Cultural Revolution, the American pop artist, Andy Warhol, made the picture one of his multiple-image silk screen prints. It is perhaps some measure of Mao's current reputation that at an auction in Beijing in 2006 the original painting by Zhang Zhenshi, which was priceless at the height of Mao's power, sold for the equivalent of £90,000.

Astonishingly, in view of the god-like position Mao once held in China, many young Chinese born in the 30 years since his death in 1976 know little about him. They recognize him as an icon but have no great understanding of what he did in China. Schools and universities devote little attention to his career. Few television documentaries now deal with him; the emphasis in education and the media is on the future not the past. Youngsters are more likely to meet his image in a club or disco where Mao look-alike competitions vie for popularity with Elvis Presley impersonations.

03

the Cultural Revolution, 1966–76 – China's time of madness

This chapter will cover:
- the motives behind the Cultural Revolution
- the scale of suffering
- the destruction of Chinese culture
- the legacy of the Revolution.

China's collective hysteria

Between 1966 and 1976 China went mad. In that decade it became convulsed by the Great Proletarian Cultural Revolution, a movement launched by Mao Zedong during which the mass of the Chinese people abandoned rationality and engaged in a sustained orgy of killing and destruction. They humiliated, beat and killed anyone suspected of being opposed to Mao and razed or burnt the shrines, temples and works of art of pre-Maoist China. Why? The extraordinary answer is because Mao told them to. The people were so in awe of him and were so convinced that everything he said was true and everything he did was right that few questioned the morality or worth of his instructions.

In seeking to understand this mass hysteria, commentators have used such terms as brainwashing and coercion. These certainly help as explanations, but there was more to it than that. In the early years of the Cultural Revolution the people were possessed by a pervasive sense of euphoria. There was a universal feeling among the Chinese that they were engaged in a great collective enterprise that was elevating their nation to the highest level of worth that was humanly possible. This feeling was recaptured in the recollections of some of those involved. 'We felt that we were defending China's revolution and liberating the world.' 'Mao was divine, and the revolutionary tides of the world rose and fell at his command.' 'You felt you would give Chairman Mao your everything – your body, your mind, your spirit, your soul, your fate. Whatever Chairman Mao wanted you to do, you were ready to do it.'

Some Chinese who participated in all this later asked themselves shamefacedly how it could have happened. How could they have been so gullible and so violent? Lo Yiren, who as a teenage girl had been a Red Guard, later lamented: 'We were worse than beasts. At least beasts do not slaughter their own kind.' But the great majority of the perpetrators are reluctant to talk about it. It is the victims who are the most willing to recall the time of madness. Deng Pufang, the son of Deng Xiaoping, had his back broken and was left permanently crippled after Red Guards hurled him from a window. He commented: 'The Cultural Revolution was not just a disaster for the Party, for the country, but for the whole people. We were all victims, people of several generations. One hundred million people were its victims.' Harry Wu, who spent 20 years as one of Mao's political prisoners, said that 'everybody in China had either been a victim or knew someone who was: When the Red Guards were running around like madmen, it wasn't really a case of us-against-them. It was us-against-us. You could call it a class war, but it was worse. It was Chinese savaging Chinese.'

Mao's reasons

Why did Mao Zedong deliberately start a movement which brought misery and suffering to his people? One answer is that he was an old man. In 1966 he was aged 73 and had begun to count the days left to him. He was in fact to last another ten years, but by 1966 had begun to sense his mortality. His fear was that the revolution he had created would be betrayed after he had gone. Hence his determination that before he died he would leave China so permanently marked that it could never be changed. He had come to believe that many of the leaders in the party and government had gone soft. 'They eat three meals a day and fart. That's what Marxism-Leninism means to them.' The comforts of office and position that they enjoyed had turned them into 'neo-capitalists'. They had lost their sense of revolutionary purpose: 'The officials of China are a class, and one whose interests are antagonistic to those of the workers and peasants.'

As with many leaders who have held absolute power, there was a marked element of paranoia in Mao. The more powerful he became, the more he feared that opposition to him was growing. He feared that factions in the party were preparing to overthrow him. The fact that they did not openly challenge him made the position worse since their silence and apparent conformity made it difficult to hunt them down. His answer, therefore, was to mount a massive purge of the party, one so extensive that it would expose all the betrayers, faint-hearts and toadies, who could then be removed in a great act of purification.

Although he had acknowledged no guilt for the failure of the Great Leap Forward and the fearful famine it had produced, he knew his reputation had been damaged. That was the reason he had kept out of the limelight since 1962, leaving Liu Shaoqi and Deng Xiaoping with the task of bringing the famine to an end. But the prestige they had gained from successfully doing this had made him jealous and resentful. Liu and Deng were now marked men. The Cultural Revolution would be a way of getting back at them. Mao was driven by jealousy of his popular colleagues and a twisted vision for China. The methods he used belonged to the tradition that had shaped him personally and his nation historically – the violent removal of opposition.

The Cultural Revolution also fitted in with an idea that Mao had promoted since his earliest days as a Communist. He had always argued that revolution was not a single event; rather it was an unfolding process involving constant struggle. He now judged that the smug and complacent party bureaucrats had lost their appetite for the struggle. So what was needed was a major shake-up that would get rid of the time-servers and restore to the Communist Party the urgency and purpose that had carried it to power in 1949. To do this, he planned to bypass the party bureaucracy and enlist the Chinese people in a giant campaign that would destroy the reactionaries and save the revolution. The campaign would be deliberately terrifying and disruptive. Only by the harshest means could it be made successful. In one of the contradictions in which Mao loved to deal, he spoke of 'great disorder across the land leading to great order'.

Mao was also determined not to allow China to go the way of its great rival, the Soviet Union. In his eyes, the USSR had betrayed Communism by being too liberal at home and too willing to come to terms with the capitalist nations of the West. Mao's term for this was 'revisionism'. It was the term he would now apply to the policies followed by those he wished to destroy in China. Nobody in the party or government was safe.

There was also a strongly nationalistic element in Mao's thinking. It has been said of the Chinese that they do not really have an ideology, only a love of China. That certainly applies in this context. Mao was determined to reassert the revolution he had led as an expression of China's unique greatness. He wanted to throw off any foreign influence that had crept in, whether Western or Soviet. Whatever the cost, Mao wanted China to go it alone, to follow its own path.

The cult of Mao

Mao could not have embarked on such a gigantic enterprise had the ground not already been well prepared. To the great mass of the Chinese people Mao Zedong by the mid-1960s had become little less than a god. This was the result of a massive propaganda exercise organized by Lin Biao, head of the People's Liberation Army (PLA), and the man nominated by Mao as his successor. Lin had skilfully projected the image of Mao as the saviour of the nation and the living embodiment of all that was good in China. Mao was the voice of truth and the great benefactor of the people. His picture was everywhere and his words were quoted constantly in the media and on public hoardings. Lin's most effective piece of public relations was to produce *Quotations of Chairman Mao Zedong*, known to China and the world as 'the Little Red Book'. This publication first appeared in 1964. Its bright red plastic covers, between which were selections from Mao's speeches and writings, made it the most instantly recognizable book in the world. It became China's bible, an appropriate analogy since its preface opened with the exhortation, 'Study Chairman Mao's writings, follow his teachings and act according to his instructions'. And the Chinese people did exactly that. In its first four years, sales of the Little Red Book topped 750 million. Everyone carried a copy; it fitted into school children's satchels and workers' lunch boxes. Readings from it settled every dispute and preceded every organized public event. Mao was the source of all knowledge and wisdom. He was the new Confucius, though nobody dared say this.

Another incident brilliantly exploited the deep-rooted Chinese notion that appearances matter. In July 1966 Mao, who had not been seen in public for four years, suddenly showed up – swimming down the Yangzi River. It was a cleverly stage-managed affair that captivated the Chinese. Newspapers and newsreels were full of it for weeks. The message was obvious: the Chairman was as strong and purposeful as before. He had swum in the Yangzi, the great river that symbolized China's life force. Mao Zedong was back.

The attack on 'revisionism'

The immediate prelude to the Cultural Revolution was an official announcement in April 1966 that the CCP had been infected by 'revisionism'. There had been discovered within its ranks 'a sinister anti-party and anti-socialist line that is diametrically opposed to Chairman Mao's thought'. To stifle this before it could wreak untold damage, the PLA had been brought in to lead China in rooting out the 'anti-socialist weeds'. With a swift switch of metaphors, the party called on the people of China to join in the attack on all those who were daring to endanger the revolution by 'taking the capitalist road'. Panic set in as every official rushed to declare his absolute loyalty to Mao and the party. They were too late. By the high summer of 1966, all those in the party and government whom Mao suspected of being opposed to him had been removed or demoted. The way was now open for the most intensive terror campaign any society has ever undergone.

The August rally, 1966

The Cultural Revolution first came to the attention of the Chinese people as a whole and to international observers on 18 August 1966. On that date Tiananmen Square in Beijing filled with a million people, who over the course of the day shouted and screamed themselves into peaks of ecstasy whenever Mao intermittently appeared on a balcony of the Forbidden City overlooking the Square. He did not himself address the crowds that day; he left that to mortals. Lin Biao was the principal speaker. He described Mao Zedong as an incomparable genius, who was 'remoulding the souls of the people'. Acting on Mao's bidding, Lin appealed to the throng to commit themselves to an attack on the 'four olds'. This was Mao's designation for those forces of conservatism – 'old thoughts, old habits, old culture, old customs' – that had produced the revisionists who were now threatening the nation and had to be wiped out.

The fascinating and ironic aspect was that the majority of those venerating Mao in the Square that day in the first of what was to be a series of giant demonstrations were youngsters in their teens and early twenties. The 73-year-old Mao, worried over his longevity, had selected the young to be the instruments of the Cultural Revolution. It was a shrewd choice. Mao calculated that if he could enlist the enthusiasm and energy of the young they would be a formidable force. The desire for acceptance by their peers is a characteristic of the young in all cultures. Mao played upon this powerful sense of conformity by inviting the youth of China to band together in the systematic destruction of people, artefacts and values that he now deemed obsolete. In private conversation he remarked: 'We have to depend on them to start a revolution. We must liberate the little devils. We need more monkeys to disrupt the palace.'

The young, who took up Mao's challenge as eagerly as he had hoped, were not being wholly naïve. It is true that he was using them in a calculated and cynical way but they had good reason to follow him. Mao's eminence in China was more than just a matter of incessant propaganda and clever public relations; it was based on real achievement. The young people who chanted 'Chairman Mao, may you live for a thousand years!', and sang 'Mao Zedong is the red sun rising in the east' were paying homage to the most successful leader in Chinese history. As they saw it, China under him had broken free from Japanese occupation and Western domination, had overtaken the Soviet Union as the head of international Communism, had developed its own nuclear weapons, and had become a super-power capable of matching the USA.

He had done all this, moreover while leading a great social and political revolution within China itself. In idolizing Mao for this, the young were reverting to two traditional attitudes in Chinese society – emperor worship and social conformity. This was another reminder that Confucian values had survived in Communist China. Yet the extraordinary paradox was that Confucianism was condemned as belonging to the four olds that were marked for destruction. Indeed, the name Confucius was tagged on to anyone or anything the Maoists wanted to condemn, as in 'the Liu-Deng-Confucius clique' and 'Confucian, capitalist revisionism'.

The Red Guards

The young responded to the appeals made to them at the great rallies by rushing to become Red Guards. This was the movement specially created by Kang Sheng, the head of Mao's secret police, to act as terror squads. Wearing distinctive armbands, units of Red Guards were to be found in every major area. Taking as their watchword Mao's slogan 'It is right to rebel', they set about destroying the four olds. The first target was the education system. Teachers and lecturers were dragged from classrooms and lecture halls and denounced as reactionaries for perpetuating the myths and superstitions of the past. They soon learned that the only way to save themselves was to admit their teaching had been utterly wrong and to promise never to repeat such anti-revolutionary crimes.

Few things in society are as frightening and depressing as young people with closed minds. These young fanatics became a fearful and brutal force. In a direct inversion of the traditional Chinese respect for age and learning, the Red Guards, totally free from police interference, ran amok, attacking people at will and destroying property. They commandeered public transport and took over radio and television stations. When some party members grew anxious over the excesses of the Red Guards, Mao specifically ordered that no restrictions were to be placed on them.

Growing ever more arrogant and vicious, the Red Guards broke into houses to hunt down anyone showing signs of 'decadent tendencies'; this definition included the wearing of Western clothes or make-up, and the possession of books of a non-revolutionary kind. The discovery of private altars or shrines was enough to prove that the householders were enemies of the people; they and their neighbours were forced to watch as the home was ransacked and the offending articles smashed to pieces or burnt. No building, no matter how antique or how loved by the locality, was exempt from attack and vandalizing. Temples, libraries and museums were obvious targets.

The assault on the intellectuals

A group that the Red Guards took particular pleasure in terrorizing was the 'intellectuals', a term stretched to encompass all those whose way of life or work was judged to have given them privileges denied to the people. Teachers, writers, artists and even doctors were branded as 'bad elements' or 'class enemies'. Wearing large dunce's caps and with their crimes written on pieces of cardboard hung about their necks, they were publicly paraded and forced to confess that they had abused their positions of privilege.

Those who dared to resist were subjected to special 'struggle sessions'. These involved arrest, deprivation of sleep, and a never-ending demand from teams of accusers that the individuals accept their guilt. As part of the process for breaking the spirit of the victims, they were put into the 'aeroplane' position – head pushed down, knees bent, hands together, and arms pulled high behind the back. This was accompanied by punches and kicks and a continuous volley of verbal insults. Few were capable of surviving more than a day or two of this. But giving in did not bring the victims relief. They had to write a confession, the first draft of which was always rejected. They had to accuse themselves of more and more crimes. Only when they had produced a totally abject self-denunciation was the torture relaxed. As many as 23 Beijing University staff members were so shattered by such treatment that they took their own lives. Even in death they did not escape the contempt of the Red Guards whose term for suicide was 'alienating oneself from the party and the people'.

The removal of Liu Shaoqi and Deng Xiaoping

Enjoyably vindictive though the humiliation of the intellectuals was, Mao was after bigger fry. As the pro-Mao demonstrations in Beijing grew more intense and the Red Guards increased their levels of terror, Mao turned directly against Liu Shaoqi and Deng Xiaoping. Both men were removed from their government positions for having taking 'a bourgeois reactionary line' and for supporting 'Soviet revisionism'. Wall posters appeared accusing them of 'betraying Maoist thought'. Liu was frogmarched from his house and subjected to a series of brutal 'struggle sessions'. He was then held in a cramped cell and denied treatment for his diabetes. When he eventually died in 1973, he had been reduced to a skeletal figure lying in his own filth. Deng Xiaoping escaped with his life but only after being forced to stand in public while 3,000 Red Guards screamed abuse at him. He was then sent to perform 'corrective labour' in Jiangxi province in 1969.

Mao played little part in directing the Cultural Revolution once it had begun. He withdrew from Beijing leaving Lin Biao and Jiang Qing to run things. Lin and Jiang kept the pressure on by providing the Red Guards with the names and whereabouts of suspect officials and party members. The government compound off Tiananmen Square, which housed the offices and apartments of ministers and officials, was put under siege. Day and night the Red Guards, armed with loud-hailers and amplifiers, maintained a non-stop assault on the ears of those trapped inside. 'Minister Chun and wife of Minister Chun, show yourselves. Do not try to hide, you dirty rightists and revisionists!' Such insults constantly and ear-piercingly repeated became intolerable for the besieged. As if that were not enough, search lights were beamed onto the windows at night, making sleep impossible for those inside and reducing them to quivering hysterics. Those who tried to maintain some sort of normality in their lives by leaving the compound were easy targets for the besiegers who formed terrifying gauntlets through which the official and his family had to push. The mocking Red Guards were only too eager to turn their insults and jeers into physical assault.

Red Guard in-fighting

Beijing was naturally the centre of Red Guard activity, but groups of these youngsters appeared everywhere in China. As so often happens with revolutionary movements, splits began to appear within the Red Guard ranks. Regional and local rivalries led to savage in-fighting as groups tried to establish through force that they were the true revolutionaries and their opponents were revisionists. Violent clashes that resembled a form of tribal warfare were a common occurrence. In Harbin, for example, a large city in Northern China, opposed factions, all claiming to be fighting in the name of Mao, engaged in a blood bath in which hundreds of thousands died. The students did not have it all their own way. Tired of being dictated to by callow youths, factory workers formed their own Red Guard detachments. Vicious fighting followed as the competing factions vied for supremacy.

The role of the PLA

Yet these disturbances, disruptive and deadly though they often were, should not be described as anarchy. Maoists always claimed that the Red Guards were a spontaneous movement, but that was never the case. The Red Guards were the creation of Mao's secret police and from the first they were under the control of their creators. If the civilian police and the PLA had chosen to interfere, the Red Guards would have been powerless. They were allowed to run riot only as long as it suited the Maoist authorities. The role of the People's Liberation Army was crucial in this respect. As the successor of the Red Army, the heroic force that had carried Mao to power, the PLA had a special place in his affections. Mao knew that his political authority rested ultimately on the loyal support of the military. As he was fond of saying, 'all power grows out of the barrel of a gun'. For their part, the PLA never wavered in their loyalty to him. That was why, having let the Red Guards take the initiative in the early stages of the Cultural Revolution, the PLA then moved in and took control. Army units travelled throughout China imposing their authority on the Red Guards and forcibly dispersing them when they showed reluctance to give up. This did not mean the end of the violent campaign against 'the class traitors and enemies of the party and people'. If anything, the severity intensified as squads of the PLA took over from where Red Guards had left off in hunting down and terrorizing 'counter-revolutionaries'.

The dispersal of the Red Guards

Faced with millions of young people who now had no outlet for their energies, Mao's government embarked on another massive social experiment. A great appeal went out to the youngsters to go 'up to the mountains and down to the villages'. There they could help the peasants by learning 'the dignity of labour' and sharing the life of the rural poor. The government's aim was not simply to redirect the idealism of the young but more cynically to disperse the throngs of troublesome youths who had infested the cities in the wake of the Cultural Revolution. The trick worked; between 1967 and 1972 over 12 million young people moved from the towns into the countryside. It proved a bitter experience for most of them. Few adapted well to the harsh conditions and they were not welcomed by hungry peasants, who were unwilling to share their meagre food supplies with patronizing students who knew nothing about farming. Intense homesickness and near-starvation were the common lot of the youngsters. Many of them said later it was this experience that first made them question the sincerity and truth of Maoist propaganda.

Mao's determination to reshape Chinese culture

Savage though the political side of the Cultural Revolution was, it is at least understandable as a bitter power struggle for the leadership of China. What is more difficult to grasp is why it was so necessary to involve so many innocent Chinese. That puzzlement is even greater in relation to the specific aspect that gave the Great Proletarian Cultural Revolution its full name. Mao Zedong aimed at nothing less than the transformation of Chinese culture. For Mao, culture was not something additional to society, a matter of refined interests and tastes relating to the arts. It was an expression of the values, attitudes and practices by which a society defined itself. Its culture was all that made a society what it was. It was a totality. It followed that art in all its forms – music, theatre, sculpture and painting and so on – must directly represent the values of the society in which they are produced. Culture takes its form from the values of the predominant class. The culture of a feudal society was feudal, of a bourgeois society bourgeois, of a socialist society socialist. In Mao's judgement, China's culture had been feudal under the emperors and then bourgeois under Chiang Kaishek and the Nationalists. Now it was his duty as leader of Communist China to use the power that he had built up since 1949 to make the PRC a truly proletarian society. He would do this by ridding the nation of all those feudal and bourgeois remnants that held it back from achieving its true Communist character. This would not be easy. Class enemies would resist fiercely. There could be no half measures in dealing with them. They would have to be totally crushed. The Cultural Revolution could not be other than a violent affair. Mao had an expression for this: 'the more brutal, the more revolutionary'.

The role of Jiang Qing

In an interesting move Mao appointed his wife, Jiang Qing, to oversee the creation of the new proletarian culture. She was given the responsibility for making the arts in China conform to a political programme. The 'four olds' were to be eradicated in the arts in the same way as they were being destroyed in the political field. Jiang brought a vindictive fervour to her role as censor-in-chief of all the art forms. All works for public performance or showing had to be submitted to her for approval. Her rigidly enforced rule was that any creative work, whether it be in the field of literature, music, painting, sculpture, theatre, radio, television or cinema had to be directly relevant to the lives of the workers. Only contemporary, socially realistic themes were acceptable. There was to be no ambiguity or hidden messages in the work, nothing abstract. The story or plot had to concern itself with the triumph of the peasants and workers over evil landlords and capitalists. Western music, whether classical, jazz or pop was ruled out totally. In an extraordinary decision, traditional Chinese opera, despite being one of Mao's great loves, was also banned. It was replaced by a repertoire of eight opera-ballets dealing with the glorious victories of the masses over their class enemies. These repetitive and unimaginative productions numbed the minds and bottoms of the audience who, nevertheless, greeted them with rapturous applause lest they be accused of a lack of class consciousness.

Jiang was not content merely to issue orders. She had the habit of dropping in unannounced on rehearsals for plays or operas. She was a terrifying presence, barking out instructions, dismissing performers or directors who displeased her, and demanding re-writes. Her aim was to destroy any sense of respect for China's past and its traditions. Anything that could be labelled bourgeois came under attack. Nothing had intrinsic worth any longer. The value of everything was to be judged by whether it promoted or retarded Mao's socialist revolution. The only truth was socialist truth, the only beauty was socialist beauty. Traditional artistic values were dismissed as being decadently reactionary and bourgeois. Since all art was a form of propaganda intended to maintain the rule of the dominant class, it was nonsense to talk, for example, of a beautiful painting or a beautiful piece of music. The painting and the music were the products of a bourgeois culture constructed by the suppressors of the people.

As a practical demonstration of the new cultural thinking that Jiang was attempting to inculcate, school children were encouraged to trample over lawns and stamp on flowers to show their contempt for bourgeois ideas of beauty. Schools were in the front line of the war against the corrupt culture of the past. Pupils were trained to throw off sentimental family ties. A Beijing student recalled that from his first day at school, aged seven, he was taught that he had to love Mao more than his own parents. 'I was brainwashed for eight years and looking back I realize that the party was purifying us so we would live for Mao's idealism, Mao's power, instead of discovering our own humanity.'

The destruction of culture

China's music schools and academies were subjected to particular attention. Instead of studying scores, the students now studied the thoughts of Chairman Mao. Music was no longer heard. Instead of practising, the students put aside their instruments and sat in 'self-criticism' groups confessing that they had betrayed Mao's revolution by learning the corrupt compositions of the foreign bourgeoisie or by performing the decadent music of China's feudal past. Teachers and students won applause when they declared that from now on they would play only works of revolutionary integrity. Those who were dubious about accepting the new ways had a hard time of it. It was common for suspect students to be exiled to paddy fields, where they were given no tools and forced to work with their hands, the aim being to ruin the sensitivity in their fingers so that they would never play well again.

Similar treatment was meted out to any creative artists who dared resist the new orthodoxy being created by the Cultural Revolution. They were sent to prison camps to be 're-educated'. The official myth was that they were not being punished but helped towards enlightenment by being introduced to the dignity of labour. So pervading was the fear that such tactics generated, that there was no organized resistance to Jiang. Reprehensibly, if understandably, politicians and artists kept their silence, hoping that once the ageing Mao had died, Jiang's tyranny would end.

The result of Jiang's policies was that by the mid 1970s China was a cultural wilderness. It is always easier to destroy than create. Artists either stopped working altogether or simply produced works that were distinguished only by their dull conformity to the official line. Creativity ceased. The damage done was summed up in the 1980s by a Chinese poet, Yan Yen: 'As a result of the Cultural Revolution you could say the cultural trademark of my generation is that we have no culture.'

The Cultural Revolution – the final phase

The Cultural Revolution did not fully end until Mao's death in 1976, but by the early 1970s it had begun to lose some of its ferocity. In part this was because serious doubts about it had crept in among some Chinese. These were unspoken, of course. While Mao was still alive, his authority went unquestioned. However, behind the scenes an undeclared power struggle had begun in the party that would come out into the open once Mao had passed on. What stimulated the private questioning of the Cultural Revolution was the strange fate that befell Lin Biao. In 1971 Lin was killed when his plane crashed in Mongolia while he was trying to flee from China. He had been implicated in a plot to assassinate Mao and he was trying to escape arrest. That was the official version of events given when the announcement of his death was finally made over a year after it had occurred.

The truth behind what happened has never been fully established. It is open to question whether Lin had really plotted against Mao or whether Mao concocted the story so as to have a pretext for removing him before he grew too popular. As significant as the death itself was what followed. Once the news had been announced, a virulent attack was launched on Lin's reputation. He was denounced as 'the great traitor and Soviet spy' and the people were asked to join in a 'criticize Lin Biao and Confucius' campaign to show that they understood how reactionary Lin had been.

Here was an extraordinary turn of events that baffled many Chinese. Lin Biao, the inspiration behind the Little Red Book, the honoured leader of the PLA, the creator of the cult of Mao, and the man Mao had nominated to succeed him, had been revealed as a betrayer of his country and the would-be assassin of his leader. It beggared belief. People became sceptical. They asked themselves how trustworthy were the leaders of the Party in which such things could happen. A village elder summed it up neatly: 'When Liu Shaoqi was dragged down we'd been very supportive. Mao Zedong was the red sun and what not. But the Lin Biao affair made us see that the leaders up there could say today that something is round; tomorrow, that it's flat. We lost faith in the system.'

The legacy of Mao's Cultural Revolution

Various estimates have been given for the number of Chinese who were killed during the mayhem of the Cultural Revolution. Some figures are more trustworthy than others, but the general consensus is that the death toll ran into millions. Grim though the details are, it is worth quoting some of the more reliable statistics. In the capital Beijing in 1966, the first year of the Cultural Revolution, 1,700 people were battered to death. Some of these were arbitrary killings by mobs in the streets. Others were more organized affairs; bound victims were dragged off to sports grounds or stadiums where they were systematically clubbed to death in front of excited spectators. A variant on this form of killing, usually applied to those who struggled rather than meekly submitted, was to pour boiling water over the victims until they died of shock. There were authenticated cases of people being choked to death by having iron filings or nails forced down their throat. In the public square of Daxing County, a suburb of Beijing, the locals were treated over a two-day period to the spectacle of 300 people having their brains knocked out with bats and clubs. Between 1966 and 1975 there were 67,000 killings in Guangxi province while the figures for Mongolia, Tibet and Sichuan in that decade are reckoned to be in hundreds of thousands. The purging of the Communist Party cost the lives of over half a million CCP officials.

The deadly legacy of the Cultural Revolution was that it appeared to legitimize fanaticism and brutality provided it was carried out by the government. Acting with an absolutism that out-matched that of the emperors, Mao, on what was no more than a whim, plunged China into turmoil and disruption. He deliberately created an atmosphere of violence in Chinese society in order to pursue his personal vendetta against members of the party. Of course, having introduced the Cultural Revolution he depended on others to implement it. So many Chinese were complicit in the imposition of terror. Yet the main focus must be on Mao Zedong himself. As a revolutionary, Mao thought of people in terms of their class, not their individuality. It was this attitude that explains why he could follow a policy without compunction, whose consequences were death and suffering for millions of his people.

It may yet prove that the Cultural Revolution has left a permanent mark on China. It was a terrifying example of what Chinese leaders are prepared to resort to in times of a real or perceived crisis. It belongs to the violent tradition that has characterized the development of modern China. Hitler killed his people because of their race, Stalin killed his people because of their class, Mao killed his people because of their thoughts. In the grim league table of horrors of the twentieth century, Mao's treatment of China ranks at the top. Six million European Jews were killed in the Nazi Holocaust, 25 million Soviet people were destroyed in the purges that disfigured the USSR during Stalin's era. But, if the numbers of Chinese who died in the persecutions of the 1950s, the famine of 1958–63 and the Cultural Revolution of 1966–76 are added together, the lowest estimate of the death toll is 50 million, the highest 100 million. These are figures that defy imagination and confound explanation.

04

the Deng Revolution, 1979–89 – China joins the modern world

This chapter will cover:
- China's handling of Mao's legacy
- the Deng Revolution
- the democracy movement in China.

Deng Xiaoping

Within two years of Mao Zedong's death in 1976, a man took over at the head of Chinese affairs who in his own way was to prove as remarkable a leader as Mao. Having survived denunciation and exile during the Cultural Revolution, Deng Xiaoping returned to become the dominant force in China until his death in 1997. Deng was to achieve a change in the nation's policies that truly merits the term revolutionary. If any one person could be said to have created modern China it would be Deng.

Between 1976 and 1978 Deng was able to outmanoeuvre the other contenders for power, including Jiang Qing and her main supporters, known as the Gang of Four, who were arrested and imprisoned. Deng had three main strengths. One was his popularity with China's armed forces and the provincial leaders of the CCP. A second was his successful record as an economic planner; he had been the main figure in the ending of the famine in the early 1960s and had worked with Zhou Enlai in the 1970s in drafting 'the four modernizations', a major programme for national economic recovery. A third asset was Deng's standing as an international statesman. While Mao Zedong had been the figurehead in China's foreign policy, Zhou Enlai had been the minister who had actually operated it between 1949 and 1976. Deng had been Zhou's principal assistant for much of this time, gaining a reputation as a skilled and subtle representative of his country. This was very evident in 1978 and 1979 when Deng personally led separate Chinese delegations to a number of Asian countries, including North Korea and Japan. He also became the first PRC leader to visit the United States.

The Third Plenum 1978 – the PRC's turning point

Once Deng had become the dominant member in the Chinese government, he set about introducing the new policies he wanted China to follow. Deng's honorary title was 'paramount leader'. This had no defined powers attached to it, but in an odd way this increased his authority. He had deliberately avoided accepting any formal position because he did not want to be tied. He knew he could rely on his influence and connections to remain in charge of affairs.

Deng, a diminutive figure scarcely five foot tall, was now in a position to begin what, without exaggeration, has been called 'the Deng Revolution', a process that was to reshape China and turn it into the economic giant it has now become. The first momentous step was a CCP meeting in 1978. At this gathering, known as 'the Third Plenum', he began the process of restructuring post-Maoist China. The meeting resolved to 'restore party democracy' by reinstating those who had been wrongly condemned during the Maoist purges of the 1960s and 1970s. In effect, this was a declaration that the Cultural Revolution was finally over. The Plenum also gave authority to Deng to pursue his four modernizations – the reform of agriculture, industry, defence and education.

Keen though he was to discard Mao's economic and social policies, Deng Xiaoping was too shrewd to launch an all-out attack on Mao's legacy. Mao had been a god to the Chinese people and Deng judged that they would not easily adjust to the idea that he had been a failure. Moreover, any criticisms of Mao would by implication be an attack on those who had carried out his policies, which included all the current leaders of the CCP. It was far more prudent, therefore, to let Mao's reputation gradually fade than directly undermine it. A CCP statement, written by Deng Xiaoping himself, declared: 'It is true that Mao made gross mistakes during the Cultural Revolution, but his contribution to the Chinese Revolution far outweighs his mistakes.' The party subsequently produced a very neat equation that said that Mao had been right in 70 per cent of his decisions and wrong in 30 per cent of them. This left Deng and the government free to abandon Mao's policies without its ever becoming an issue.

Deng's economic reforms

Deng had already shown his basic approach in the 1970s. He was essentially a realist in economic matters. Whether it was in agriculture or industry, he argued that if a scheme worked it should be kept; if it did not, it should be dropped. Even in Communist China, policies should be dictated by results not by economic theory. If trade with the capitalist West could help sell China's goods, then such contact should be promoted. Deng's pragmatism was expressed in one of his celebrated sayings: 'It doesn't matter whether a cat is black or white, so long as it catches mice.'

Deng stressed that this approach would strengthen not weaken China's communist character. In 1982 he said his policies for stimulating the economy at home and opening China to the outside world were designed to develop the socialist economy. But while 'socialist public ownership will always remain predominant, the aim of socialism is to make all people prosperous'. The state would not entirely detach itself from economic planning but much greater freedom would be granted to the local managers who were actually doing the job. The planners and bureaucrats in Beijing would be the servants not the masters of the Chinese economy.

Deng's four modernizations programme started from the conviction that Mao had been misguided in thinking that China could make itself economically self-sufficient by controlled central planning. If China was to become prosperous it needed to restore the market and open China to foreign commerce.

Agriculture

In the countryside, the much-hated system of communes, which had been set up by Mao in the late 1950s and which had been a major cause of the famine, was ended and the original villages were restored. The peasant farmers could once again hold land and farm for profit. The government also introduced a subsidy policy to protect peasants against poor sales of farm produce or falling prices. The result of these changes was that farm output improved significantly. Grain and rice production rose from 300 million tons in 1978 to 440 million tons in 1992. In the same period meat production went up from 9 million to 29 million tons.

However, the picture was not entirely rosy. Despite the benefits brought by privatization and subsidies, the peasants were still unsure about their property rights. In most cases privatization had not granted permanent ownership; after 15 years the land would revert back to the State. The government promised to extend the leases, but the peasants were not convinced; they had long memories of being betrayed by government promises throughout the century. Their doubts tended to deter them from improving their farms or adopting new agricultural techniques. The result was that the peasants, conservative by nature and tradition, declined to embrace the government's plans for modernization and expansion.

Industry and commerce

A point to stress, and one that explains many of China's present problems, is that although agriculture was one of the four modernizations it was very much a secondary consideration for Deng and the government. Their principal concern was the development of industry and commerce. In the PRC's economic planning, priority would always be given to these. The same approach applied to education, Deng's third modernization. Education was not seen as something idealistic that existed for the improvement of the individual; it was the means by which the nation would acquire the skills and know-how to create a great modern industry that would allow China to compete with the world. That is why the emphasis was on scientific education and training. Higher education was central to this. Reversing Mao's destructive policies that had closed the universities during the Cultural Revolution, these were now expanded in size and number. One million technical students were trained as managers and administrators of the new economy. A big push was given in this direction by sending thousands of Chinese students to study abroad. The obvious aim was for them to gain knowledge of successful Western industrial technology. It was not intended that they should imbibe Western political values, though this, to the later embarrassment of Deng's government, is what sometimes happened.

Once back in China, this new managerial class became the vital element in the development of the Special Economic Zones (SEZ). These were areas containing China's main export industries, which were now selected for intensive industrial development. The first four were Shantou and Xiamen in the north, and Shenzen and Zhuhai in the south. They were given regional independence and granted special tax concessions. The SEZ proved to be one of China's modern success stories. Between 1981 and 1991, Chinese exports grew by over 500 per cent. By the early 1990s China's trade was in balance and foreign investment in China had quadrupled.

The progressive feature that Deng brought to his policies was his willingness to reward economic success even when it had been achieved by ignoring Communist economic theory. Deng was greatly impressed by the way young managers rejected the anti-capitalism of traditional Maoism and instead operated by the basic rules of common sense. The managers had both raised manufacturing output and improved the quality of products by introducing incentive schemes. Workers received higher wages if they learned new skills and turned out better goods. Profit was no longer a dirty word in Communist China.

This new attitude brought its shocks. Workers had grown accustomed to the 'iron rice bowl'. This was the term given to the system that had operated under Mao by which companies were subsidized and workers received guaranteed wages. In Mao's time, industries had been brought under direct central control; production targets, prices and wages had all to be fixed by the State. Since any surpluses a subsidized company might make went straight back to the State, there was little point in a company being efficient. By the same token, there was no incentive for the workers to make any effort since whether they were conscientious or idle they still received the same wages. This protection of companies and the workforce destroyed any sense of endeavour. But though none of this made economic sense it did provide the workers with a job for life. Now, however, Deng's enterprise policies were going to end the workers' security. They had lost their iron rice bowl, which had included welfare benefits for them and their families. Workers would now have to earn their wages or face dismissal. Freedom from state control for companies also meant the end of their state subsidies. Companies would have to become efficient or go under.

It was little wonder, therefore, that Deng's programme of modernization met opposition from those affected. This was why the reforms took far longer to put into operation than had been planned. It is true that in the 1990s government schemes were introduced to give the workers some measure of protection but even in the middle of the first decade of the new century barely one-tenth of China's industrial workers were covered by such schemes. Yet, whatever the problems that accompanied Deng's revolution, the basic truth was the reforms he had initiated had provided the basis on which a modern industrial complex began to rise, one that promised to make China one of the world's greatest economic powers.

Deng's opposition to political reform

Striking though Deng's modernization agenda was, one reform was deliberately omitted. There was to be no political change in China. At his death in 1997, an English newspaper referred to Deng Xiaoping as 'China's last emperor'. It was a fitting description. He had used his influence to redirect China on a new path and he had done so from the top. China would follow where he led. Deng's revolution belonged to the Chinese tradition in which change was inaugurated by the central authority with little reference to those below. His revolution had left out politics; nothing was to change on that front. The absolute rule of the Communist Party was to remain intact. He stressed that the modernizing of the economic system did not mean the liberalizing of the political system. The four modernizations were to be accompanied by the 'the Four Cardinal Principles'. Deng defined these as 'keeping to the socialist road, upholding the people's democratic dictatorship, upholding leadership by the Communist Party and upholding Marxism-Leninism and Mao Zedong Thought'. In 1980, under his guidance, the Party had formally condemned the notion that the people 'have the right to speak out freely, air their views fully, and hold great debates'. Deng always insisted that China's first need was for internal stability; modernization was impossible without this. Those Chinese and foreign outsiders who urged China to move towards some form of western democracy were deluded.

Deng's aim was to restore the morale and authority of the CCP after the disruption of the Mao decades. Whatever his progressive views on economics, in politics he was a Communist hardliner. Like Mao Zedong, he was part product, part creator, of the turbulent history of China through which he had lived since the 1920s. His belief in the absolute right of the Chinese Communist Party to govern China was unshakeable.

But when a government that claims absolute power decides to introduce reforms, even though they are limited to economics, it is taking a great risk. The decision by Deng to modernize China's economy, while at the same time denying political freedom to China's people, created tensions that were to have a terrifying climax.

The growth of the Chinese pro-democracy movement, 1979–89

Until it was razed by the authorities in the 1990s, a brick wall ran 250 metres along the Avenue of Eternal Peace, near Tiananmen Square. In the late 1970s the Avenue became a common gathering place for students, who started the practice of sticking messages on the wall. These began harmlessly as adverts and lovers' notes but quickly became a way of publicly criticizing the Communist Party and government. Every so often, the authorities stepped in, tore down the offending posters from the 'democracy wall', and made arrests. In 1979, Wei Jingsheng, a former Red Guard, used the wall as part of his personal campaign to challenge the government over its failure to introduce genuine democracy into China. Wei was grabbed off the street and given a 15-year prison sentence.

Wei was the first victim to suffer on behalf of 'the democracy movement'. This was never an organized party. It was more a loosely structured pressure group of the 'intelligentsia', those academics, journalists and lawyers who had been originally excited by the thought that Deng's abandonment of Maoism marked not only the modernizing of the economy but also the beginning of political liberty. Initially, the democracy movement did not oppose the government or the CCP. Instead it urged that the party, which claimed to believe in the rule of the people, should put its belief into practice by extending political freedoms. It accepted Deng Xiaoping's 'Four Cardinal Principles', but pleaded that a fifth one should be added – democracy. For Deng's government this was a demand too far. The intelligentsia had to be shown a lesson, hence the severe punishment of Wei Jingsheng.

What the authorities were at their touchiest over were suggestions that they had become corrupt. In the late 1970s a damaging court case in Heilongjiang province had revealed that the managers of a fuel and power company had been embezzling state funds on a huge scale. The culprits were tried and shot in public. The government had ordered the trial and executions as a way of winning popular approval for its firm stand against racketeering. But its action had the opposite effect. It emerged that the government had intervened only after the scandal had first been exposed by a probing journalist. More damaging still was the revelation that the criminals in the Heilongjiang affair had all been top members of the provincial Communist Party. A feeling began to spread that there was something corrupt at the core of the CCP's management of China.

It was such scepticism that fuelled the series of student demonstrations that occurred in the 1980s. University campuses became the main sites of protest. The demand made by the demonstrators was for greater political democracy and economic opportunity. In 1986 thousands of students followed Fang Lizhi, a professor at Hefei University who also happened to be a prominent member of his local Communist Party, in calling for the authorities to honour the commitment to open government that was written into the PRC's constitution. In this instance, the protests were crushed by the dismissal of Fang and the arrest of the student leaders. But despite its claim that the protesters were an unrepresentative bunch of troublemakers, the government had been alarmed. This was evident from the swift demotion of Hu Yaobang, the CCP General Secretary, who, his colleagues felt, had encouraged the students to protest by openly suggesting that political change might be allowed. Deng Xiaoping at this point restated his basic line that modernization did not mean moving towards western-style democracy. Once the 1986 protests had been dispersed, he reminded government and party that the only acceptable and workable system in China was 'democratic centralism', the enlightened rule of the Communist Party. 'The people's educational level,' he claimed, 'is too low for anything else to work. Without the leadership of the Communist Party, there can be no building of socialism.'

Deng's political thinking

Deng's reactionary attitude needs to be understood. He had lived through the turmoil and horrors of the anti-Japanese struggle, the civil war between the Nationalists and Communists, the Great Leap Forward and the Cultural Revolution. This experience had convinced him that stability was now China's greatest need. He further believed that stability could be achieved only by retaining the socialist system in China. Deng once said that China suffered from too much politics, by which he meant too much political theorizing. For him, socialism was less important as a revolutionary ideology than as a practical system for preserving China from disintegration.

Yet it was becoming clear by the late 1980s that Deng's attempt to ride two horses was causing mounting frustration among the progressives in China and within Deng's own government. His policy of pursuing economic and commercial reform while at the same time trying to prevent any political change made conflict more not less likely. This duly came in June 1989 in the form of the Tiananmen Square massacre.

05

repression and expansion – China, 1989–97

This chapter will cover:
- the Tiananmen massacre
- political repression under Deng
- Deng's legacy to China
- China's recovery of Hong Kong.

2–4 June 1989

It is traditional in Asian countries to use water canon to disperse protesters, but not on this occasion. The government was determined to teach the bitterest lesson possible to the young people who were defying them. By 2 June, 350,000 crack troops of the People's Liberation Army had Tiananmen Square surrounded. Now there was no way in or out. The troops' orders were 'to reclaim the Square from the rebels at all costs'. The 'rebels' were unarmed students. Tanks and armoured half-tracks moved into position. At 10 pm on the night of 3 June the first shots rang out. The demonstrators ran for cover but there was none. Shooting continued on and off throughout the night and into the morning. By midday on 4 June the six-week occupation of the Square was over. Thousands lay dead and injured. A massacre had taken place. Those who had survived it were marched away for interrogation and imprisonment. In the reprisals that followed, CCP officials who had shown sympathy for the protesters were dismissed, while those who had resisted the demonstrators were promoted.

The Tiananmen Square massacre in June 1989 has a significance beyond its own time. It provided a commentary on all that had happened in China since Mao's death and exposed the underlying political problems that modern China has yet to solve. How had it come about that China was willing to shoot its young?

The road to Tiananmen Square

Despite the success of Deng Xiaoping's schemes for China's industrial and commercial expansion, by the end of the 1980s there were many who felt let down. The disappearance of the iron rice bowl left many people very vulnerable. China's ever-increasing population and the continuing movement of people from the country to the town made accommodation in the urban areas scarce and kept living standards low.

The democracy movement became a focus for economic and political disappointment. Students considered that, despite the promise of progress and reform, the party under Deng Xiaoping had failed to deliver. A common grievance among the students was the lack of career prospects. As part of the four modernizations programme, many more students had entered higher education in the late 1970s. Yet it was evident a decade later that the number of worthwhile jobs on offer was far below the number of graduates wanting them. Adding to the sense of resentment was the realization that the jobs that were available were reserved for CCP members. It was another example of party corruption.

Matters began to build towards their tragic climax in April 1989 with the announcement of the death of Hu Yaobang, the former CCP Secretary. His dismissal by Deng in 1986 for showing sympathy towards the democracy movement, followed by ill-treatment that hastened his death from a heart attack, had endeared him to the students. They now elevated him into a martyr who had died defending democracy. Large crowds had gathered in Tiananmen Square on the day of Hu's memorial service. They demonstrated noisily as three kneeling students begged Premier Li Peng to accept a petition from them as he made his way into the Great Hall of the People for the ceremony. Li's pointed refusal to take the petition confirmed the protesters' belief that the government had lost touch with the people. There followed a series of sit-ins and boycotts of university classes. *The People's Daily,* the official CCP newspaper, cranked up the tension by denouncing such actions as rebellion by 'a small handful of plotters'. An editorial warned, 'If we are tolerant of, or conniving with, this disturbance and let it go unchecked, a seriously chaotic state will appear', which would destroy all that had been achieved under the four modernizations. It urged that the rebellion must be crushed.

Rather than deterring the students such threats spurred them to greater efforts. Groups from over 40 universities in China rushed to join a demonstration in Tiananmen Square. Zhao Ziyang, the Party General Secretary, attempted appeasement by publicly stating that *The People's Daily* had gone too far. But the demonstration in the Square had begun to gather pace; hundreds of the protesters began a hunger strike. In the middle of May the government tried to defuse the situation by making direct contact with the student leaders, the first time it had acknowledged them. It appealed to the students to end the hunger strike and leave the Square.

But the students refused. Circumstances, they believed, had put them beyond the reach of the government. Their demonstration was now receiving international press and television coverage; foreign camera crews and journalists as well as students were encamped in the Square. The students calculated that the

Chinese government would not dare to use force against them in such a situation. They also judged that events had created an even stronger check on the government's freedom of action. Mikhail Gorbachev, the Soviet leader, was about to arrive in Beijing on an official visit. That was why the international media was in Beijing. The demonstrators reckoned that while he was present in China the government would not risk moving against them. It was a naïve calculation. While it was true that the authorities did nothing while Gorbachev was in China, once he had gone they felt free to act. Angered by the embarrassment the students had brought to China by their presence in the Square during Gorbachev's visit, the hardliners in the government were determined on a showdown with the protesters.

The day that Gorbachev left China, Zhao Ziyang, one of the few pro-student ministers still in the government, went down to the Square to address the protesters. Moved to tears by his knowledge of what was in store for them, Zhao begged them to disperse. Li Peng also spoke to the students, but briefly and coldly. The reality was the government had already made the decision to use violence to end the demonstration. In preparation for this, Li Peng made a broadcast branding the students as 'rioters' and declaring that 'the fate and future of the People's Republic of China are facing a serious threat.' It was a wild exaggeration, of course, but it supplied the pretext for Li to announce that the government was about to take 'firm and resolute measures to end the turmoil'.

This stark announcement rallied the students, some of whom had begun to have doubts, into a last-ditch stand. They voted to continue their occupation of the Square. Arguably this is precisely the response the government wanted. Had the protesters meekly dispersed, this would have taken away the justification for the punishment that was prepared for them and denied the government the chance to show how resolute it was in defending the PRC from its internal enemies. In the end, the student defiance played into the government's hands. So it was that on the night of 3–4 June, the demonstration was crushed in blood.

The lesson of the massacre

The pitiful remnants of the occupation with its sodden sleeping bags, bedraggled banners and broken plaster replicas of the

Statue of Liberty bore pitiful witness to the grim fact that Communist China was not yet willing to contemplate democracy. The violent suppression of the protest was a statement by the Communist leaders of the PRC that they would allow no challenge to their power. In this regard the massacre was entirely in keeping with the tradition of Chinese rulers using the most ruthless means against those who dared confront them. It was something the emperors and Mao Zedong would have perfectly understood.

China after Tiananmen

The Tiananmen massacre confirmed that the new era reforms introduced under Deng Xiaoping had not altered the political structure of the PRC. It remained an authoritarian Communist regime. Yet there were strains within the government and party. Deng was aware that what he called a left and a right had developed within the CCP. By the left he meant those who were unhappy about the speed with which China was embracing economic liberalism, those who would have been quite content to see the PRC less advanced as long as it kept its Communist character. By the right he meant those in the party keen to move even faster towards economic growth, towards 'total westernization'. Deng saw it as his task to hold a balance between these two for if either influence became too strong it could destroy what had been achieved by his reforms. In a sense, Deng had defined the problem that still confronts China's leaders today – how to modernize the nation and at the same time be true to the principles of Chinese communism.

By the early 1990s this had become an even more difficult conundrum. The velvet revolutions that brought down the Soviet-dominated eastern bloc countries and eventually the Soviet Union itself suggested that Communism was a spent political force. But where did that leave Communist China? Should it cling to the belief that it was a leader of international revolution or should it return to China's traditional view of itself as a unique culture separate from all others? Of one thing Deng was sure: China could not detach itself from the world economically. Its survival as a nation depended on its capacity to produce and to trade.

Deng's political attitudes

Deng Xiaoping was a realist and a pragmatist. His own bitter experiences during the GMD-CCP civil war, the Great Leap Forward and the Cultural Revolution had convinced him China's greatest need was stability. He further believed that the only way to preserve that essential stability was by retaining the Communist system in China. Communism, for Deng, mattered less as a revolutionary ideology than as a practical system for preserving China from internal chaos and possible disintegration. Communism was the new Confucianism; it was a set of common values that, if adhered to, enabled China to function as a harmonious society. It followed, as it had in Confucian times, that anyone who dared to disrupt that harmony, were deserving of the severest treatment that the State, the guardian of society, could impose.

Continuing repression under Deng

It was because he was, in the Chinese context, a political conservative that Deng Xiaoping presided over an increasingly repressive regime. At his death in 1997 there were more political prisoners held in China than there had been in 1976 at the time of Mao's passing. By the late 1990s the People's Republic of China was running a prison-camp system, known as the 'laogai', that was larger than the notorious gulag that had operated in the Soviet Union under Stalin. Harry Wu, a pro-democracy activist who served 20 years in various labour camps within the laogai described it as 'the biggest concentration camp system in human history'.

Another notable victim of Deng's regime was Wei Jingsheng who, in 1979, had been the first martyr in the government's crackdown on the protests that began at the democracy wall in Beijing. Wei's original sentence of 18 years was increased by another 14 years in 1993 for 'subversion'. His crime this time was speaking out against the government while he was in prison; in June 1989 he had condemned it for its massacre of the demonstrators in Tiananmen Square. Wei was the type of political dissident who showed up the essential fraudulence of the Communist Party's claim to be the party of the people. At the time of his second sentence in 1993, *The Observer's* Hong Kong correspondent wrote: 'Wei is the nightmare scenario made flesh, the man who more than anyone else proves Beijing to be incapable of tolerating dissenting views, even if they are peacefully expressed'. Wei was eventually released in 1997. This was not an act of remission, but simply that the Chinese authorities did not want the embarrassment of Wei, who was chronically ill, dying in prison.

Deng Xiaoping's final years

Deng died in 1997 at the age of 92. The Western press referred appropriately to the passing away of the last emperor of China. For a number of years before his death he had not played an active part in public affairs, but his was still the dominant influence in the Chinese government. Indeed, it is possible to say that he remains the greatest influence on Chinese affairs since none of the leaders who have followed him have diverged from the twin policies he bequeathed to China – modernization of the economy accompanied by an implacable refusal to grant political freedom to the people. He failed by just five months to see his last great diplomatic triumph come to fruition – the official takeover by China of Hong Kong. The manner in which he reached that success is worth considering since it tells us a great deal about his view of China's place in the modern world and in international affairs. Deng's policies had in effect created 'two separate Chinas that now existed in parallel'. He had taught that China could combine a policy of 'one nation, two systems', that it could modernize its economy and open itself to the outside world while at the same time retaining the absolute authority of the CCP in politics.

The PRC and Hong Kong

In the nineteenth century Britain had acquired the colony of Hong Kong in three separate stages. The colony was never just one single place; it was composed of three separate areas – Hong Kong island, Kowloon, and the New Territories. In 1842, after the Opium War, China by treaty granted Britain the island of Hong Kong on a permanent basis. In 1860 Britain formally added Kowloon, the harbour directly facing Hong Kong, to its permanent possessions. The third piece of territory, Kowloon peninsula, in which the harbour stood, was gained for Britain in 1898. This last piece, known as the New Territories, was not granted to Britain in perpetuity but only on a 99-year lease.

figure 2 map of Hong Kong

The British Crown Colony of Hong Kong so formed in 1898, was to develop during the following century into one of the most prosperous cities in the world. After the Communist takeover of mainland China in 1949 it became a haven for those fleeing from Mao Zedong's authoritarian PRC. Thousands of businessmen and bankers, who brought their wealth with them, settled in Hong Kong and quickly turned it into a world centre of manufacturing, commerce and finance. By the 1970s a cleverly marketed tourist industry began to add to the island's prosperity. Hong Kong was a boom town.

Its impressive feats produced a mixture of resentment and admiration in China's communist rulers. Nowhere in the PRC was there anything to match Hong Kong's capitalist economic miracle. Yet, the PRC could take deep satisfaction from the thought that under the terms of the 1898 agreement, Hong Kong, 'the pearl of the orient', would return, with all its riches, to China in 1997. Deng Xiaoping anticipated that it would add a huge asset to his modernization plans for China.

But would things go to plan? Polls showed that 95 per cent of the Hong Kong people wanted to stay British. Would Britain be willing to honour the letter of an old treaty and hand over the colony and its people to a repressive Communist regime that was capable of such madness as the Great Leap Forward and the Cultural Revolution? In strict legal terms, Britain had a case for not doing so. According to the earlier treaties, Kowloon and the island of Hong Kong were permanent British possessions. It was only the New Territories that were leased. The PRC expected to meet difficulties and prepared for a long diplomatic battle. But to its surprise, Britain seemed willing to make concessions in the Sino-British talks that began in 1979. Margaret Thatcher, the first British Prime Minister to go to China while in office, was personally involved in the negotiations from 1982 onwards. Her evident keenness to reach a settlement encouraged Deng Xiaoping to take a hard line. He told Mrs Thatcher that the PRC regarded Hong Kong as a part of sovereign Chinese territory and there was no question of Britain's lease being extended. 'I would rather see Hong Kong torched than leave Britain to rule it after 1997,' he told her.

Britain was not in a strong bargaining position. The idea of giving up the New Territories but keeping Hong Kong and Kowloon was not really an option. It was the New Territories that supplied Hong Kong with its essential water and power supplies. The logistical and geographical problems of supplying the island by any other means were insurmountable, as were the difficulties of defending it militarily from the Chinese. Deng was not exaggerating when, in one sharp exchange, he told Mrs Thatcher that Chinese forces 'could walk in and take Hong Kong later today if they wanted to'.

Deng's strength was not simply logistical. He felt he also held the moral high ground. His argument was that, whatever the legal niceties involved, Britain's claim to Hong Kong was founded on dated imperialist concepts. The British had originally acquired the colony in the nineteenth century only through bullying and coercion; they had used their superior military strength to force China to sign away Hong Kong against its will. It was, said Deng, an example of colonialism at its most exploitative. As *The People's Daily*, the mouthpiece of the CCP, put it: '150 years ago, to maintain its drug trafficking in China, Britain launched the aggressive Opium War against China, during which it carried out burning, killing, rape and plunder on Chinese soil.'

The Joint Declaration, 1984

Aware of its military and moral weakness, all Britain could work for was a compromise that would give Hong Kong some form of legally-binding protection after it returned to China. This came in the form of the Sino-British Joint Declaration, signed in December 1984. Britain agreed that on the expiry of the lease on the New Territories in 1997 all the areas that made up Hong Kong would return to the possession and authority of the PRC. For their part, the Chinese Communists declared that Hong Kong after 1997 would be treated as a 'Special Administrative Region' (SAR) until 2047. This would leave its capitalist economic structure unaltered. Deng Xiaoping described the co-existence of the Communist mainland with the capitalist island as 'one country, two systems'. He added, 'When we speak of two systems, it is because the main part of China, with a population of one billion, is practising socialism. It is under this prerequisite that we allow capitalism to remain in a small part of the country. This will help develop our socialist economy, and so will the policy of opening to the world.'

The arrangement under which Hong Kong would operate as a SAR was known as the Basic Law, which would smooth the transition of the ex-colony to full incorporation into the People's Republic. Britain and China seemed happy with the agreement they had reached; the Hong Kong people, however, still had grave doubts. Events were soon to justify their concerns. In June 1989 came news of the Tiananmen Square massacre. If the Communist government could order the shooting of its own people, asked Hong Kong democrats, would it worry about a little thing like keeping to the terms of the Joint Declaration?

Hong Kong's democrats

The Tiananmen tragedy threatened to cast a shadow over relations between Britain and Communist China during the eight years leading to the 1997 handover. Difficulties arose. One principal cause of dispute was Britain's attempt, directed after 1992 by Chris Patten, the last Governor of Hong Kong, to introduce as much democracy as possible into Hong Kong before Britain left. One tactic that particularly incensed Beijing was Patten's attempt to turn Hong Kong's Legislative Council (LEGCO) from an appointed body into an elected one. The PRC government made it clear that as soon as it took over in 1997 it would reverse this move and replace LEGCO with its own

Nominated Legislative Council. The PRC's anger over this issue was not entirely unreasonable. The truth was that Britain, during its previous 150-year control of the colony, had made no attempt to introduce democracy into its governing of Hong Kong. All holders of official positions had been appointed by the British, not elected by the Hong Kong people.

While Hong Kong's democrats applauded Patten's efforts, the British government were lukewarm in their support of him. While careful never to contradict him openly, the Foreign Office let the Chinese know that Britain did not really intend to put problems in their way. Indeed, much to the bitterness of the colony's democrats, Britain seemed intent on causing as little fuss as possible by not pressing Beijing on the democracy question. British diplomats appeared to have overcome the concerns about China that they had experienced in 1989 over the Tiananmen Square incident. There were critics of British policy towards China in the period before the Hong Kong handover who believed that Britain, having negotiated the 1984 Joint Declaration, simply could not wait to be rid of the colony. Since the thing was now inevitable why continue to make trouble over it? There were more important matters Britain should be looking towards. Among these was the maintenance of good relations with China whose billion plus population offered huge commercial prospects for Britain.

There were also notable figures in Britain who believed that China needed to be shown more understanding. Edward Heath, a former British Prime Minister and a frequent visitor to China, urged people in the West not to be censorious or superior when considering Chinese attitudes. He argued that the very different histories of China and the West made it inappropriate to judge the two cultures by the same standards. It was unreasonable, therefore, to expect Beijing to apply Western forms of democracy in Hong Kong or any other of its territories. It should be added that the democratic parties in Hong Kong found Heath's analysis highly objectionable. They dismissed it as typifying the reasoning that allowed Britain's officials and ministers to keep their consciences clear while selling out the Hong Kong people to a repressive regime.

Hong Kong today

Just how repressive that regime would prove to be in Hong Kong was the big question asked at the time of the 1997 handover. A decade later the question has still not been fully answered. In July 2006, on the ninth anniversary of that event, 60,000 Hong Kong pro-democracy demonstrators took to the streets in what has become an annual protest. They carried banners that read 'JUSTICE, EQUALITY, DEMOCRACY'. The slogan was intended to draw attention to the way in which Beijing has steadily increased its influence in Hong Kong's affairs. The main grievance is that Beijing has indeed carried out what it threatened to do in response to British attempts to introduce democracy in the 1990s; it has used its power of appointment to the Legislative Council to put in office pro-Beijing personnel, while keeping out members of the Hong Kong Democratic Party.

Yet, on the surface, the PRC has kept to the main terms of the Basic Law and SAR arrangement and treats Hong Kong as a special region. It has to be noted that for every anti-Beijing protest march there is a pro-Beijing one. It is true that the latter are organized by the government and do not match the numbers who turn out for the former, but it does suggest that there may be a greater degree of harmony than Beijing's critics allow. This may be the message to be taken from the principal speaker at the July 2006 pro-democracy rally. Anson Chan, a veteran protester, declared, 'Today I came to take part in the march, but this doesn't mean we are trying to challenge the government.' This seems to indicate a willingness to accept the idea that since Beijing is the ultimate authority it is better for Hong Kong's democrats to try to persuade it than to oppose it.

A factor that encourages co-operation rather than confrontation is that economically Hong Kong continues to flourish. To be sure, there are pockets of poverty and deprivation, but these existed when the island was a colony. Overall, Hong Kong has not suffered the decline that many forecast would happen after 1997. As long as it remains prosperous, the political challenges to the new Hong Kong are unlikely to become rebellions. The consideration that puts all the protests and manoeuvrings into perspective is Hong Kong's ultimate destiny as a fully integrated part of China. This is unavoidable and it makes Beijing's attempt to increase its influence there understandable, even if regrettable. It is unrealistic to expect that the PRC would simply allow one of its richest cities, whatever its strange history, to meander along for 50 years as if it were not a part of China.

06

Tibet – the land of the snows

This chapter will cover:
- China's takeover of Tibet
- Tibet's separate character
- the great famine in Tibet
- the Chinese attempt to destroy Tibetan culture
- Tibetan resistance
- the PRC's current exploitation of Tibet.

Since it came into being, the People's Republic of China has laid claim to Tibet as part of China. The PRC's case is a very poor one. Historically, Tibet had never been Chinese. Its culture, its language, its religion, its ways of life and its geography make this most westerly region of China, the land of the snows standing on the rooftop of the world, a distinct and separate entity.

A description was given in Chapter 02 of the appalling famine that afflicted the rural provinces of China between 1959 and 1963. The deepest misery occurred in Tibet. There, one-quarter of the four million population died. The sickening aspect of this fearful toll was that the Chinese authorities did not merely tolerate the famine in Tibet; they actively and deliberately made it worst. It was an act of genocide. Whereas it could be claimed that the famine elsewhere was a consequence of faulty planning, cock-eyed science and half-baked political and social theory, in Tibet the tragedy was exploited by Mao Zedong to intensify the suffering of the Tibetan people.

Chinese hatred of Tibet

The beginnings of this tragedy go back to 1949. One of the first acts of the new Communist regime was to assume authority over the whole of China, including those border regions which had always resisted control by the central Chinese government. Ignoring Tibetan claims to be an independent people, Mao asserted that the region was a part of the sovereign territory of the new communist state. In 1950, he ordered crack units of the People's Liberation Army (PLA) into Tibet to achieve 'reunification'. This was a euphemism. What it meant was that Tibet's separate identity was to be destroyed.

The invading PLA met with spirited defiance; 60,000 Tibetans joined the fight to preserve their land and culture. But the struggle was hopeless. The Tibetans did not have a regular trained army, and such weapons as they possessed were no match for the fire power of the PLA. Within six months open resistance was crushed. The occupying army then began a reign of terror. A systematic programme was introduced to obliterate the culture, the language, the religion of Tibet – in short, everything that gave definition to the Tibetans as a people. Tibet was renamed Xizang, and protesters were rounded up, and either imprisoned or executed.

Having gained military control of the region, the Chinese government over the next ten years consolidated its hold by sending migrants from central and eastern China to settle in Tibet. The aim was to flood the conquered region with Han settlers whose numbers would swamp the indigenous community. Chinese lifestyle was imposed as the norm, and local peoples who tried to cling on to their traditional ways were imprisoned.

The 1959 Tibetan Rising

But it is not easy to kill off a culture. Tibetan resistance went underground in 1950 and for a decade managed to keep alive the flame of resistance. This defiance was invariably met with ferocious reprisals. In 1959 the resistance movement was courageous enough to organize public demonstrations against the Chinese occupation. The PLA brutally suppressed the protests and followed this with a terrifying assault on the Lama (Buddhist) faith, perhaps the outstanding expression of Tibetan identity. Priests and nuns were expelled from their ancient Buddhist monasteries, and publicly ridiculed and beaten. Mention of the Dalai Lama, the Tibetan spiritual leader, was forbidden.

Systematic destruction

By 1959, famine had begun to spread across central China. It provided the perfect pretext for the Chinese to complete their destruction of Tibetan resistance. Pretending that the mounting number of deaths were the result of bad weather and outdated farming methods, the authorities insisted that the new 'socialist' farming techniques be adopted by the Tibetans. The Chinese famine need not have spread to Tibet. The grim fact was that it was interference by Chinese officials, pursuing Mao's agricultural policies, that lethally destroyed the food production system and plunged Tibet into death and misery.

Traditionally Tibetan farming was one of two kinds: nomadic herding and barley growing by resident farmers. For centuries this had been sufficient to meet Tibet's needs. The Dalai Lama made this point strongly: 'When we heard there was large-scale famine, it was a new thing. Famine was unknown in Tibet. In Tibet food supplies had been sufficient for centuries. Agriculture was old-fashioned but sufficient.'

Destruction of the pattern of farming was the Chinese way of enforcing the PRC's grip on the rebellious region. The barley farmers were forced to switch to other crops such as wheat and maize. These proved highly unsuitable. Not only did they not grow well in the high plains of Tibet, but even when a crop was harvested it proved impossible for the Tibetans to eat it. Customarily, they consumed their barley in the form of a paste called *tsampa*. Attuned to this practice, their digestive systems could not cope with the harshness of wheat or maize. The result for many was chronic diarrhoea, dehydration and death. In a further official assault by the Chinese, the nomads of Tibet, known as *Khampas*, were forbidden any longer to roam the pasture lands with their herds. With the deliberate aim of destroying this traditional way of life, the authorities forced the *Khampas* into communes where they died or eked out an existence of utter misery. Writing in 1961 at the height of the distress, Huo Shi Tang, a *Khampas* woman, described the horror of it all:

> Every day five or six people were found dead every morning. The bodies of the children and old people were always swollen with hunger. Since most men had been arrested, about 60 per cent of the adult population were women. We would collect grasses from the fields, boil them and force this mixture down our throats. If you didn't, then you would die. But you had to keep an eye out for the guards. If they caught you, then they would grab you by the throat and choke you to make you spit out the grass seeds. There were also special teams which searched people's home for grain, digging up the floors, breaking open walls and looking through the fodder for the horses. The searches went on all through the famine. If they discovered any food, even a few grains, then they would organize a big meeting of 500 or 600 people. The guilty would be paraded round, beaten and spat on. Some people were beaten to death.

In a further refinement of what amounted to mass torture, those *Khampas* who were allowed to keep their herds were told they were no longer nomads but farmers. An official Chinese report that later leaked out, noted: 'They were forced to start farming the high pastures. Old and young were yoked to the plough because their yaks were not domesticated and so could not be trained to plough a field. The officials had to make them do this otherwise they would be disregarding Mao's orders.'

The *Khampas* were also instructed to follow the socialist science of animal rearing. Disregarding the importance of the yak herds on which the Tibetans depended for their food and clothing, the experts from Beijing refused to allow the herds to be moved from the communes to summer or winter pastures. Supplies of food stuffs rapidly dwindled. Deprived of their regular source of milk, cheese and meat and without the yak hair to make clothing and tents, Tibet's nomads died in droves from malnutrition and cold. In another notorious example, the Chinese officials dictated that the native Tibetan mountain sheep were to be crossed with Ukrainian sheep. Rather than strengthening the stock, the cross-breeding merely weakened the sturdy Tibetan strain with the result that few of the newly bred sheep survived the winters. It was small wonder that in 1959 the *Khampas* provided the Tibetan resistance movement with some of its most dedicated and heroic members.

The Dalai Lama

The severity with which the 1959 rising was suppressed by the PLA led to the flight of the Dalai Lama. In 1959, he chose to leave the country rather than wait for his inevitable removal by the Chinese. This was not cowardice. The Dalai Lama was willing to die for his faith and his country. But he was persuaded that as an exiled but free man he would be better able to voice the plight of the Tibetan people to the outside world. In exile the Dalai Lama became a potent symbol of Tibetan resistance. It was through him that the world's media were kept informed of the inhumanity of the PLA's occupation. To its eternal credit, India granted sanctuary to the Dalai Lama. In the face of bitter protests from Beijing, Pandit Nehru's government allowed him to make his permanent home in Sikkim in northern India.

The Panchen Lama's report

It was the Panchen Lama, deputy to the Dalai Lama, who stayed to record and publicize the horrors of the famine. In 1962, following a secret tour of Tibet, he sent Mao a 90,000-word report accusing the PRC authorities of having engaged in genocide. So grim was the story the Panchen Lama told that were it not corroborated by hundreds of personal accounts by the victims, it would be barely credible. One eye witness from a commune in northern Tibet recalled:

My brothers went around picking up whatever food they could find. Sometimes they found bones, which might have been human, and ground them into a kind of paste, adding barley husks. We did not have *tsampa* but we ate this instead. We had to work very hard and were very hungry. Many people died at this time.

In another region, a monk described how two-thirds of the local men were arrested without charge and sent to a labour camp where 70 per cent of them died. He added:

Those who remained at home had to work from early morning until night. People were frightened to talk, in case they were called counter-revolutionaries and beaten. Many people were beaten. No one could leave the commune. There had been enough food but it was taken away by the Chinese.

Another monk noted that the Chinese guards took particular delight in making the lives of the imprisoned monks hell. Of the 400 monks dragged from one monastery less than 100 survived their captivity.

The Panchen Lama's method as he travelled Tibet was to ask in each region where he stayed how many persons had been arrested, imprisoned, executed or starved to death. His final calculations showed that around 20 per cent of the population had been gaoled, an average of between 80 and 100 for each village, and that half of these had died while in prison.

The Panchen Lama had been moved to write his report to confound the lies put about by the Communist authorities. He had been particularly angered by a formal statement in 1960 by the National People's Congress which referred to 'the wonderful situation prevailing in Tibet today'. He had also reacted bitterly during his tour when he saw that preparations were being made to celebrate New Year in an area where a notorious labour camp had recently stood. Did they really intend, he asked rhetorically, to dance on the graves of thousands of men who had died a horrible death?

His question had a terrible literal meaning. In another area he found that corpses of defeated freedom fighters had been dragged down the mountains by Chinese troops and dumped in a huge pit. The relatives had been forced to gather round before being told: 'We have wiped out the rebel bandits and so today is a day to celebrate. You will dance on the pit of the corpses.' The Chinese assault on the Buddhist religion of the people was relentless. Their faith was described as 'backward, dirty and useless'. What offended the Panchen Lama's religious instinct was the way in which the Chinese deliberately ignored the traditional Tibetan burial rites of the victims. Mass death was now followed by interment in mass graves. He believed that this affront to Tibetan sensibilities was a part of the deliberate humiliation of the people. 'When a person dies, if there is no ceremony to expiate his sins for his soul to be released from purgatory, this is to treat the dead with the utmost cruelty.'

Snippets from the report reveal an endless litany of brutality to which the Tibetans were subjected.

Requisitioning was brutal: nearly all the reserve food, meat and butter were confiscated. There was no oil to light lamps, not even firewood.

To survive, herdsmen had to eat many of their animals.

The people were herded into canteens where they were fed weeds, tree bark, leaves, grass roots and seeds.

A tiny infectious illness like a cold led to masses of deaths. Many died directly of starvation. The death rate was really terrible.

Such awful pain of hunger had never existed before in Tibetan history.

People were beaten till they bled from the eyes, ears, mouths, noses. They passed out, their arms or legs broken. Others died on the spot. For the first time in Tibet, suicide became a common practice.

Holy Lama scriptures were used for manure. And pictures of the Buddha and sutras were deliberately used to make shoes.

The Panchen Lama described how, at great risk, throngs of people came out to see him. In tears, they begged him: 'Don't let us starve! Don't let Buddhism be exterminated! Don't let the people of the Land of the Snows be exterminated.'

When Mao received the report, which was addressed personally to him, he refused to acknowledge its contents. He ordered that it be suppressed and the Panchen Lama, who was condemned as a 'big class enemy', was placed under house arrest. But suppression and imprisonment could not completely blanket the truth. The Chinese might condemn the report but they could not refute it. Nevertheless, they tried. The PRC's propaganda machine continued to manufacture evidence to prove that Mao's revolutionary methods were working and that stories of shortages were the work of lying counter-revolutionaries.

The truth was that the PRC were guilty of the very charge they levelled against their enemies. A survivor of the famine in Tibet wrote:

> Immediately the harvest was over, the Chinese exaggerated the results as usual. They claimed that the yield was about ten times the seed ... it followed that if we could produce a bumper crop in the first year of our 'Tibetan liberation', there was no reason why we could not double this year's yield in the following season.

Such Maoist techniques in Tibet were in tune with the way China's officials behaved throughout the famine; they denied failure and spoke only of success. The result was the death and misery of millions.

Western guilt

Sadly, the complicity of silence over the Tibetan famine was not restricted to Mao and his Communist regime. The West, too, refused to believe that it was happening. In the tense atmosphere of the Cold War, there were many on the political left who were sympathetic towards Communism but who found the Soviet brand intellectually moribund and emotionally uninvolving. They turned eagerly, therefore, to Mao's alternative form of applied Marxism. They so much wanted Maoism to succeed that they were prepared either to turn a blind eye to its failures or to put them down to prejudiced anti-Communist reporting.

The consequence was that accounts of the famine were either unreported or played down by a pro-Maoist press. Sir Alfred Sherman who, as head of an international think-tank had made a special study of Mao's collectivization programme, went so far as to assert that 'the famine was deliberately ignored by the majority of the British media'.

Continued repression under Deng

In 1965 China tightened its hold by formally declaring Tibet to 'the Tibetan Autonomous Region (TAR)'. The new title contradicted the reality that Tibet had less not more self-government. China's oppression of the Tibetan people continued through the Cultural Revolution and carried on even after Mao's death. Under Deng Xiaoping there was an apparent easing; his government tried to emphasize to the Tibetans the great advantages of co-operation. The benefits that 'reunification' could bring were dangled before them: education, health care, modern transport and an end to Tibet's backward and inefficient ways. The majority of the Tibetan people remained unimpressed. They knew that beneath the allure of such things was the same Chinese determination to intensify the occupation of Tibet and impose a stultifying foreign character upon it.

In 1985 the Tibetans' refusal to celebrate the twentieth anniversary of the TAR became the prelude to further open resistance that went on into the late 1980s. There were violent clashes when China sent in further detachments of the PLA to crush what threatened to become a Tibetan national revolt. From exile the Dalai Lama denounced China's actions in Tibet as 'cultural genocide'. To the embarrassment and anger of Beijing, his passionate defence of his benighted country led to his being awarded the Nobel Peace Prize in 1989. This was more than a recognition of the Dalai Lama's personal virtues; it was an implicit international recognition of the justice of Tibet's cause. It was also the final rebuff to Deng Xiaoping's hopes of gaining international acceptance of the PRC's Tibetan policies by persuading the Dalai Lama to end his self-imposed exile and return to his home land.

The Lhasa rising, 1993

That the PRC's terror methods had not totally crushed Tibetan resistance became evident in 1993 when the largest protest in China since the 1989 Tiananmen Square demonstration occurred in Lhasa, Tibet's capital. The same predictable Chinese response followed; the PLA were sent in and thousands of arrests were made. Those imprisoned were brutally treated. The Panchen Lama was seized by the Chinese and taken into 'protective custody', a euphemism for house arrest. Through its contacts in Tibet, 'Asia Watch', an international body concerned with monitoring human rights abuses, was able to give the Western media detailed accounts of the lethal actions of the Chinese in Lhasa. Tibetan refugees visited the UN headquarters in New York to present the horror story. Great concern was shown by the international community about China's affront to human rights but no concerted action was taken. From 1950 when it was first invaded, it has been clear Tibet lacks the strategic and economic importance to make it an area for intervention by the great powers.

Nevertheless, there have been signs in the last decade or so of a greater sensitivity on the PRC's part to international opinion. There were occasions in the 1990s and early 2000s when China responded to international pressure by releasing or reducing the sentences of those imprisoned for political offences, those described by human rights groups in the West as prisoners of conscience. The PRC did not acknowledge that it did so as a result of outside pressure and there has been no clear pattern to the leniency shown. At best, the releases have been gestures. They certainly have not been accompanied by any letting up in the authoritarian rule which China exercises over Tibet.

China's current policy in Tibet

As if Tibet's woes were not enough, in 2006 a statue of Mao Zedong, weighing 35 tons and standing 7.5 metres, was erected in Changsha Square in Gongga, Tibet. It was said officially to be a gift from the people of Changsha, Mao's birth place, responding to a request from the people of Gongga. In truth the people of neither town had any say in the matter. It was the PRC's way of further humiliating the Tibetans. The statue, carved from Changsha granite, had been deliberately shaped by its sculptor, Zhu Weijing, to combine the podgy features of Mao with those of the traditional pictures of Confucius. It represents power and authority. It is strange to think that only a generation earlier Confucius had been reviled as representing the worst of the ancient culture that had to be eradicated from China. Now here he was, the oriental sage blended with the butcher of the Tibetans. With no hint of irony, a government statement at the time of the statue's unveiling declared, 'Tibet does not need only material development. It must also meet the more spiritual needs of its people.'

The cynicism is further expressed in the way the Chinese central government now intends to exploit the region's appeal to foreign tourists. The trappings of Tibetan culture are to be brought out again. But this is a theme-park, Disney form of culture. It is all superficial. Costumes, handicrafts, calligraphy; these are safe topics. Peasants wearing their traditional brightly coloured costumes, working in the fields, herding their yaks, churning yak butter, brewing yak tea, making yak meatballs, or joining in the jolly, synchronized, community dancing in the town squares: such are the delights presented to tourists as they go on their organized heritage trails. But the Tibetans have to be on their best behaviour; they are instructed not to discuss politics or the history of Tibet. The authorities use teams of spies and informers, known locally as 'watchers', to check on the reliability of the Tibetans granted the privilege of presenting their culture to the foreign visitors. Reference to the Dalai Lama is not allowed; embarrassed laughter or feigned incomprehension greet those visitors who do not realize that such themes are off limits.

The new Beijing–Lhasa railway

It was as part of its programme to increase tourist access to Tibet and to encourage commercial expansion there that the Chinese government undertook the building of a railway to connect Tibet to the rest of China. The first train journey from Beijing to Lhasa took place in July 2006. In the traditional Tibetan greeting, young girls placed white scarves on the shoulders of the passengers who had made the two-day, 2,500 mile journey. As a feat of engineering the railway, which cost £2.3 billion to construct, rivals the Three Gorges project. Over a five-year period, 30,000 workers, many brought in from outside Tibet, carved their way through mountains, bridged valleys and drained swamps to lay the line. All this at a height that makes Tibet one of the hardest regions on earth in which to perform physical labour. At its highest elevation the line runs through the Tanggula Pass, over 5,000 metres above sea level. So rarefied is the atmosphere of the region that the luxury tourist hotels, which have been opened in Lhasa and Shangri-La, routinely provide their guests with face masks and canisters of compressed air.

The railway is, of course, intended as a very visible expression of Beijing's determination to consolidate its hold over Tibet. The Dalai Lama condemned it as another step in the 'cultural genocide' that the PRC has systematically imposed on Tibet. His fear, which is shared by all Tibetan nationalists, is that the railway will increase the flow of non-Tibetan migrants into the region. He described the construction of the railway as being 'politically motivated to bring about demographic change'.

This indeed is a deliberate aim of the government, which subsidizes the fares (the cheapest one-way Beijing–Lhasa ticket in 2006 being just £25) as an incentive to migration into Tibet. Nevertheless, the Chinese government has already begun to boast of the benefits the railway will bring the Tibetans, who are expected to gaze on the construction with awe and drink in the message of progress that is reinforced by giant posters that appear at key points along the line. But in putting up the inspiring posters the authorities seem to have forgotten where they were. They are written not in Tibetan but in Chinese. Hardly any of the people understand a word.

The Communist Party has not always been so unthinking. It continues its considerable efforts to convert influential Tibetans to become spokesmen for the party line. Teachers are the obvious target. If they can be persuaded or induced to commit themselves to this role it eases the government's task of subduing Tibet. Where possible, party secretaries and officials are drawn from the Tibetan population. Though regarded by Tibetan nationalists as quislings, those who do the party's bidding are well and visibly rewarded. In an example of that strange way modern China combines capitalist incentives with dated Marxist concepts of egalitarianism, the government encourages its members to buy private housing and property, all of which is intended to show the people what improvements they can bring themselves if only they will work co-operatively with the Communist party for the new Tibet. An official from Beijing illustrated the party's ability to square the circle by claiming that its Tibetan policy demonstrated the 'great socialist characteristics and the faultless work and policies of the party. Working for the people is what our party stresses. We often say we have to focus all our efforts on governing purely for the people.'

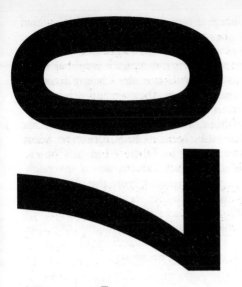

07

Taiwan – the other China

This chapter will cover:
- the character of Taiwan's Republic of China
- Cold War tensions over Taiwan
- Taiwan's economic growth
- Taiwan's relations with mainland China
- the international importance of Taiwan
- the unresolved sovereignty issue.

In practice, modern China really consists of two Chinas, the Communist PRC and Nationalist Taiwan, both, confusingly, calling themselves the Republic of China. This odd situation dates from 1949. It was in that year that, as a result of their defeat in the civil war, the Nationalists under Chiang Kaishek fled to the island of Taiwan. There they set up what they claimed was a continuation of the true Republic of China, asserting that mainland China was in rebellion against them. Mao and the Communists took the same line in reverse. Soon after his announcement of the creation of the People's Republic of China in 1949, Mao declared that Taiwan was a sovereign part of the new PRC and would be retaken from the Nationalist rebels at the earliest opportunity. Conflict seemed inevitable. Yet nearly 60 years later that conflict has still not broken out even though each side maintains its claim to sovereignty over the whole of China. In 2005, Communist China formally restated its right to take the island, by force if necessary.

The USA's involvement

Given the far greater population and resources of the PRC and the aggressive stance of China's Communist leaders on so many issues, it may seem surprising that it has not made good its threat at some point since 1949. But the PRC has not attempted to seize Taiwan for two chief reasons. One is the military problem. The PLA judged that it did not possess the necessary air power and landing craft to mount a successful invasion of the well-defended island. The second reason was that the USA committed itself to defend Taiwan. This was essentially a Cold War consideration rather than American support for Taiwan on principle. In fighting the Korean War (1950–53), the US Seventh Fleet had been sent to patrol the straits between Taiwan and mainland China and so prevent the vital islands of Quemoy and Matsu falling under Chinese Communist control. At the same time, American military advisers and supplies were sent to the Nationalists on Taiwan. In the Mutual Security Pact signed between the GMD government and the USA in 1954, the Americans pledged themselves to defend Taiwan against attack from outside.

American support did not prevent Quemoy and Matsu being shelled by PLA shore batteries, a tactic that the Communists kept up even after the Korean War was over. In 1958 the strength of the shelling suggested that a Chinese assault on

Taiwan was imminent. US vessels were also threatened in the Taiwan Strait. The USA prepared for war. But no attack came from the mainland. Communist China was not in a position to invade Taiwan and had no wish to risk war again with the USA so soon after the Korean struggle. An important consideration arises here. Although Mao Zedong publicly derided the USA and its atomic weapons as 'paper tigers', he was convinced that from the time of the Korean War onwards the USA was planning a retaliatory attack on China. He calculated that when the West was ready, it would move to destroy the PRC.

To counter this, he ordered the construction of a defensive system for China, known as 'the Third Line'. Deng Xiaoping was given the task of building a vast network of fortifications, above and below ground, so strong as to be capable of withstanding the heaviest bombardment. Deng located the Third Line in the remoter regions of central China into which, in the event of an American attack, the population and industries of the vulnerable eastern and southern provinces could be withdrawn. Since no attack came the Third Line was never completed or put to the test. The remains of some of the parts that were constructed can still be seen today, cavernous reminders of Mao's fears.

The USA's U-turn over Taiwan

During the high tide of the Cultural Revolution, the PRC denounced the USA for its 'imperialist hold' over Taiwan, which was described as being in a state of 'temporary detachment while Chiang Kaishek and his GMD rebel bandits hold the island'. However, in 1972 the historic visit of President Nixon to China eased the tension. Taiwan was one of the major questions considered at the official Sino-American talks. The outcome was that China restated its principle that Taiwan was a Chinese domestic affair 'in which no other country has the right to interfere'. The USA broadly accepted this line by acknowledging that a peaceful settlement over Taiwan could best be achieved by the Chinese people themselves. It affirmed that the USA's ultimate objective was the withdrawal of its forces and military installations from Taiwan.

The logical outcome followed. By 1979 the USA had dropped its traditional diplomatic support for Nationalist China, formally recognized the PRC and accepted its right to replace Taiwan in the United Nations. This major reversal of American post-war

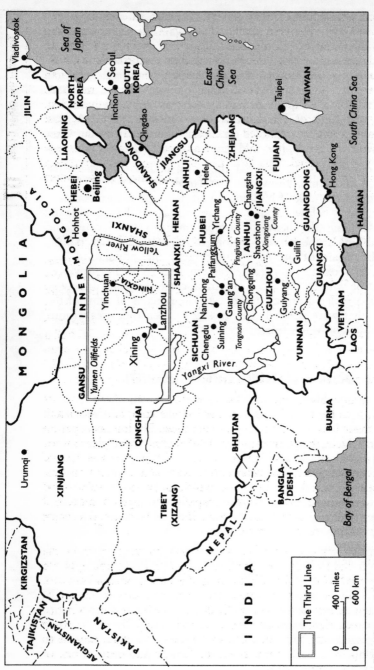

figure 3 map of China showing Taiwan and the Third Line

policy infuriated the Taiwanese who considered they had been betrayed by their one real ally. Yet, despite the shift of position by the USA, at no point had it accepted the right of the PRC to take Taiwan by force. Indeed, at the time that President Carter formally withdrew America's diplomatic recognition of Taiwan in 1979, Congress passed the 'Taiwan Relations Act', committing the USA to providing defensive arms to the island. Congress also added that any aggressive moves by China against Taiwan would be regarded with 'grave concern' by the USA. Whether this meant that the Americans would actually intervene if a Chinese attack was launched was something Communist China could not be sure of and it left the PRC's leaders permanently apprehensive.

Taiwan – the other Republic of China

Despite the Cold War tensions over Taiwan, the island itself was to be a great economic success story in the second half of the twentieth century. It achieved this initially under rigid Nationalist rule. In its early years Taiwan was no more a democracy than the communist mainland. Chiang Kaishek's government outlawed all forms of political opposition. Its half a million-strong army meant that there was little chance of open opposition being successfully organized among the island's 23 million people even though mainland agents attempted this.

The major advantage for the Taiwanese government over its great mainland rival was that the island's comparatively small size made it easy it to control and organize. The long occupation of Taiwan by the Japanese up to 1945 had not been pleasant for its people, but it had left the island with a sound economic structure in place. The Nationalists were able to build on this. Strongly backed by the USA, which provided a substantial economic aid package, Taiwan rapidly developed a successful export industry. By the early 1960s it could be counted a major international trading centre.

There were fears that when Taiwan lost its recognition by the USA in the 1970s its economy would suffer. In fact the opposite happened. Nationalist China entered a period of rapid growth, the result of effective government planning and an inflow of foreign money. It showed particular enterprise in responding to the international demand for electrical goods. By the 1990s it was in a position to commit £150 million to a giant scheme to develop the island's infrastructure. Taiwan had become one of Asia's 'tiger economies'.

Taiwan's internal politics

By the 1990s there had been equally significant developments in Taiwan's internal politics. The Nationalists remained in government but were now confident enough to allow greater democracy. Chiang Kaishek's death in 1975 helped considerably in this respect. His successor and son, Jiang Jingguo, was not as rigid in his approach. He made important moves towards the spread of local and national elections. In 1986 martial law, which had operated since 1949, was lifted. On Jiang's death in 1988, he was succeeded as president by Lee Teng-hui, a native Taiwanese. It was during Lee's presidency that the GMD formally accepted that one-party rule was unconstitutional. Interestingly, in 1991 in the first elections of the new multi-party system, the Nationalists were returned to office with a very large majority.

Lee's presidency was highly important in regard to Taiwan's relations with the PRC. Although he did not abandon Taiwan's claim to be the genuine government of the whole of China, he took a conciliatory approach towards Beijing, stating that Taiwan had no intention of 'using force as a means of seeking reunification'. What helped Lee was that, as with Hong Kong, increasing business contact was being made between Taiwan and mainland China. True this was unofficial, but it did help suggest that China and Taiwan were not, after all, irretrievably separated. This encouraged Deng Xiaoping in the 1980s to soften his line somewhat. In 1984 he said it was possible perhaps for a 'one nation, two systems' policy to exist. 'The one billion people on the mainland will continue to live under the socialist system, but a capitalist system will be allowed to exist in certain areas, such as Hong Kong and Taiwan.' But while the PRC might have softened its tone, it certainly had not shifted on the principle of the PRC's absolute right to govern the whole of China. Deng made this clear. 'Different systems may be practised, but it must be the People's Republic of China that alone represents China.'

Taiwan's fears as to Beijing's intentions were intensified by the Tiananmen Square massacre in June 1989, which clearly indicated how ready the PRC government was to resort to force in domestic affairs. Nevertheless, an interesting development occurred in the 1990s in Taiwan when the Democratic Progressive Party (DPP), which had come into being following the ending of the one-party rule, suggested that it might be possible for the Taiwanese to give up their claim to the mainland

and settle for independence for the island. It was intended as a conciliatory move towards Beijing. However, it caused divisions within Taiwan and it did not greatly alter relations with the mainland, since the PRC still maintained that Taiwan was a sovereign part of China and that independence for it could not be considered.

The sovereignty issue

The relatively easy recovery of Hong Kong from Britain in 1997 inspired the Chinese Communists to believe that the return of Taiwan was also possible. They wondered whether Deng Xiaoping's formula, 'one nation, two systems', could be applied equally to Taiwan. But that ducked the question of sovereignty. China had been able to recover Hong Kong because Britain eventually accepted the legality of the PRC's claim to sovereignty. There was no chance of the government of Nationalist China being as co-operative. Strains tightened in 2000 with the election of Chen Shui-bian as president of Taiwan. Beijing feared that, as a declared supporter of independence for Taiwan, Chen would cause trouble. This proved to be the case when Chen, following his re-election in 2004, announced that he was considering having Taiwan's constitution redrawn to enshrine the concept of the island as an independent state. Talks were hurriedly arranged between the two Chinas in the wake of this. Although Chen was prepared to drop Taiwan's claim to sovereignty over the whole of China, he reiterated the right of the island to independent status. It was at that point in 2005 that the PRC formally adopted an 'anti-secession law', giving itself the right to resort to 'non-peaceful' methods should Taiwan ever dare to take that step.

America's role

One of the major questions in the international politics of the Pacific region is how far would the USA still be willing to go to safeguard Taiwan. At the time of Taiwan's first presidential elections in 1996, the PRC ostentatiously conducted a series of missile tests. This was interpreted, as was doubtless intended, by the Taiwanese and the Americans as being China's way of reasserting its claims to authority over what it regarded as a breakaway province. The American response under President Clinton was to send a large fleet of warships to the Taiwan

Strait; his message could hardly have been clearer. However, in 1998, Clinton toned down the message by asking mainland China to understand that his earlier gesture had been solely intended to keep the peace in the region; the USA had no intention of interfering in the sovereignty dispute between the PRC and Taiwan. Clinton expressed this in the '3 Noes' formulation: no to an independent Taiwan, no to two Chinas, and no to Taiwan's becoming a member of any international body as a separate state.

Clinton's successor, George W. Bush, who became president in 2001, took a tougher stance. His State Department spoke of the USA and China being in 'strategic competition', although this did not prevent Bush from urging Taiwan to be less combatively outspoken in its dealings with the mainland.

Espionage and counter-espionage

Behind the public statements and diplomacy over Taiwan something more sinister was going on. This became evident in a number of dramatic events in June 2006. In the bamboo forest of Guangde that lies roughly midway between Shanghai and Nanjing an aircraft crashed killing all 40 persons onboard. The PRC's president Hu Jintao ordered an immediate investigation. This was no ordinary plane and the crash victims were no ordinary people. It was the most expensive and the most sophisticated aircraft China had ever put into the skies. But its value did not come from the quality of the plane itself, which was in fact a standard Russian Ilyushin-76 transporter. It was what it carried on board that made it special. The plane was fitted with the Chinese version of AWACS (Airborne Warning and Control System), the most advanced aerial reconnaissance and detection device yet devised in military history. Apart from the crew of four, all those killed in the crash were military surveillance system experts.

Since the early 1990s when the collapse of the Soviet Union left China as the world's only major Communist nation, the PRC has been trying to match the USA's military defence and espionage technology. Unable to develop this from its own resources, it has tried to buy key components and programmes. This has proved difficult since the United States puts pressure on other countries not to co-operate with the Chinese over this. But in 1999 China gained a major breakthrough when Israel agreed to sell and install its Phalcon system, which was itself based on the American AWACS. An Ilyushin-76 was bought from Russia and flown via China to Israel to be converted and fitted with the new system which would turn the plane into a state-of-the-art early warning aircraft. But this was too much for the United States, whose CIA agents had tracked the proceedings. Matters had now reached the highest level. In July 2000 President Clinton made a direct appeal to the Israeli prime minister, Ehud Barak, who was in the United States for Middle-East peace talks, asking him to cancel the arrangement with China. Barak complied; he wrote an apologetic letter to President Jiang Zemin informing him that Israel could not complete the contract and that the plane must be stripped of its equipment and flown back to Russia. This duly happened but the Chinese had not been mere onlookers while the plane had been in Israel. Before the deal was called off, a number of their specialists had been allowed to observe the installation of the Phalcon system. They had recorded sufficient detail for Chinese military experts and computer engineers to design and build China's own AWACS. More Ilyushin-76s were bought from Russia and by 2004 test flights of planes equipped with the new system were taking place in southern China.

Taiwan's espionage role

The location was significant. For decades before this the Taiwanese government had been working with the United States in developing surveillance techniques for spying on the Chinese military. The main aim was to discover the PRC's plans in regard to a possible invasion of Taiwan. It was in response to this that the Chinese were so determined to have their own AWACS aircraft which would give them a huge potential for both defence and attack. It was also why they continued to look for ways of upgrading the system. Early in 2006, Chinese scientists acquired from an American company a set of highly sophisticated radar equipment. According to the Chinese, the purchase was for legitimate use in its civil aviation programme. This was plausible since all aviation in China is under the control of the military. But there was little doubt among all informed China watchers that the radar would be used primarily to develop AWACS, particularly in regard to its attack capabilities. All the evidence points to the conclusion that the Ilyushin-76 that crashed in June 2006 was flight testing the latest modified system, hence the excitement it aroused in the Chinese military and political world.

Taiwan's continuing international significance

Clearly Taiwan remains one of the world's most dangerous flashpoints. Neither party to the long-running dispute over the island's sovereignty is willing to give way. The question is whether the PRC will at some stage exercise its proclaimed right to use force against the island. The stakes are still high. Taiwan's armed forces number nearly half a million men equipped with sophisticated hi-tech weaponry; the island is well defended and is likely to be much easier to defend than attack. It is unthinkable that the PRC would use atomic weapons against territory that it claims as its own. Nevertheless, the barely rational outbursts of violence that mar and characterize Chinese modern history should make one wary of suggesting that a further chapter in China's civil war could not be waiting to explode.

One of Deng Xiaoping's four modernizations was the upgrading of the PRC's defence system. This continues. Between 1990 and 2005 China increased its military spending by 10 per cent each year. Beijing is reluctant to give the exact figure of its arms expenditure but it is currently reckoned by outside observers to be around £65 billion. A large part of that is devoted to the development of ballistic missiles. Significantly, in 2006, some 800 of these were deployed facing Taiwan. In addition, the PRC has a cruise missile and submarine programme and an ambitious conventional arms programme. American military intelligence also reports that the Chinese appear to have given priority to the construction of landing craft. An unacknowledged but very real arms race, similar to that between the Soviet Union and the USA during the Cold War, is going on between China and the USA. The key area is the Pacific where the United States has concentrated its naval power in what it calls its 'hedging strategy'. Without naming likely enemies, it is clear that the USA sees China and North Korea as the major threats, and the likely flashpoint as Taiwan. In the summer of 2006, the USA, with contributions from Australia, Britain, Canada, Chile, Japan and South Korea mounted a huge combined RIMPAC (Pacific rim) exercise in the Pacific. It was also in the summer of 2006 that Taiwan put on its largest-ever military exercise. These were shows of strength that were clearly meant to send signals to the government in Beijing.

Taiwan's achievement

Such developments look ominous, but there are grounds for suggesting that the PRC–Taiwan dispute will not spill over into war. Over the years the island and the mainland have developed significant economic contacts. In 2006 over a million Taiwanese were working on the mainland and Taiwanese companies had invested some £30 billion in developing their businesses there. In July 2006 the start of regular scheduled airline flights between the mainland and Taiwan was a further example of increased co-operation.

Whatever the future holds, there is no questioning that Taiwan has been a great economic success story. The most striking feature to note is that Taiwan has become a democracy, albeit not the most exemplary one in world terms, but a democracy nonetheless. It has made the transition from one-party rule to multi-party politics, a process that its mainland neighbour, the PRC, is unwilling to contemplate.

08

china in the world

This chapter will cover:
- China's relations with the USA
- China's opening up to the world
- China's relations with Africa
- China's relations with her neighbours
- China's international role.

China and the USA – the parting of the Bamboo Curtain

There is a case for saying that China's entry into the modern world began in February 1972. It was in that month that the PRC overcame its fear and enmity towards the United States sufficiently for it to invite President Nixon to Beijing on an official visit to meet Chairman Mao Zedong. The idea of inviting the leader of the USA, 'the number one enemy nation', would have been unthinkable even a few years earlier. As described in Chapter 07 of this book, Mao's conviction that the Americans intended to attack his country had led him to construct the Third Line defensive system. For decades Chinese school children had began their daily lessons by chanting, 'Death to the Americans and all their running dogs'. But by the early 1970s, China under Mao was ready for a change. Without abandoning its anti-Americanism completely, China was prepared to soften its line. Odd though it may at first appear, the reasons had less to do with the USA than with the Soviet Union.

Relations between the former Communist allies, the PRC and the USSR, had plummeted by the end of the 1960s. The contest over who truly represented the international Marxist movement, personality clashes between their leaders, border disputes, and nuclear power rivalry had caused deep divisions between them. The PRC particularly resented the policy of détente followed by the USSR. It saw this attempt to draw closer to the Western powers as a Soviet move to leave China internationally isolated. The PRC decided to reverse the position. Its approach to the USA was intended to steal the ground from under the USSR. As it happened, the USA was equally ready to see the USSR disadvantaged in this way.

The result was a willingness on both the American and Chinese sides to come together at the highest level. Zhou Enlai, Mao's astute and experienced foreign secretary, and Henry Kissinger, Nixon's wily special adviser on foreign affairs, did the groundwork for the summit meeting between the world's greatest revolutionary leader and the world's most powerful capitalist. Mao was genuinely excited by the thought of meeting his American counterpart and got out of his sick bed to greet him. The visit proved an undoubted diplomatic success. Nixon and Mao got on well and there was genuine discussion and exchange of ideas.

Though Nixon was exaggerating somewhat when he later said that his visit to China had 'changed the world', it was certainly of more than symbolic importance. It had laid the basis for closer commercial contacts between China and the USA and had been a snub to the Soviet Union in the international power game. Its special significance was that it indicated that after a quarter of a century of bitter hostility China and the USA were prepared to recognize each other's viewpoint and position. This did not mean totally amicable relations for the future; basic ideologies do not change overnight and there was always the Taiwan question imposing its reality. However, as Mao had indicated during the talks, China was prepared to raise 'the bamboo curtain' and look out on the world. It had been said at the time of the fall of the Chinese empire in 1911 that it marked 'a revolution against the world to join the world'. That revolution was nearing completion.

China opens itself to the world

In the post-Mao years, under Deng Xiaoping's modernization programme, China chose not merely to look out on the world but, in Deng's words, 'to open itself to it'. He was not simply being high-minded and internationalist. He truly believed that China's future as a nation depended on expanding its commercial contacts throughout the world. China was boosted in this aim by improving relations with the USA. In 1979 full diplomatic relations between the two countries were established. Soon after, Deng went on a presidential visit to the USA where he impressed the politicians and people who met him. The gains to China's reputation which this brought were undone in 1989 when the Tiananmen massacre reminded the West that China, for all its economic advances, was still run by a government of hardline Marxists. Yet, surprisingly, in view of the international condemnation of the Chinese government for its brutality, the event did not cause long-term damage to the PRC's expanding commercial contacts with the USA. The truth is that the USA and the West generally were, and are, willing to swallow their misgivings about China's internal politics and to continue trading. The US State Department summed up the approach as 'engagement without endorsement'; it enabled the West to keep its commercial links with China while remaining critical of the violation of human rights by the Chinese government.

This might be described as a two-way shift. Both China and the West were prepared in practical terms to move away from their rigid ideological positions. China from the 1980s to the present has been willing to ignore Marxist theory and, as well as embracing capitalism at home, has eagerly traded with the world's capitalist nations. The West for its part has been prepared to ignore the illiberalism of China's Communist regime and enter fully into trading relations with it. Both West and East have adapted to the world as it is rather than as they would like it to be.

China's response to the collapse of the Soviet Union

By a remarkable twist in international history, which few had foreseen, China was left in 1991 as the world's only major Communist power. This was a result of the 'velvet revolutions' in eastern Europe which destroyed the Communist bloc and culminated in the disintegration of the USSR. The end of the Soviet Union meant that China was the sole leader of the Marxist world. The question everyone now asked was would the PRC pursue international revolution, which according to its Marxist principles it was pledged to doing. But the Chinese leaders from Deng Xiaoping to the present have been realists. They looked at the failure of the 75-year Soviet experiment, and they noted why it had failed. They saw that the Soviet system had been unable to develop a consumer economy that could reward its people for their efforts, had been incapable of reforming its agriculture so that it could feed the population, and had pursued an arms race with the USA that it could not afford: all this presided over by a Soviet Communist Party that in its later stages no longer believed in itself. The Chinese leaders have resolved not to make the same errors. They approach international questions as nationalists not Communists. They occasionally use the language of international revolution but this is a charade. They are not prepared to risk their position and China's by chasing unobtainable and highly dangerous global objectives. Their essential aim, set in motion by Deng's reforms, has been to ensure their own political survival by consolidating China's position as a major nation that has embraced modernity. That is what determines their actions in foreign affairs. The interests of international Communism as a revolutionary movement do not come into their calculations.

China in the Pacific

It so happened that the end of Soviet power provided an immediate occasion for China to impose itself on its neighbours with a display of power that could not be matched and no other country was willing at the time to challenge. The Russian Federation that replaced the USSR in 1991 decided that it would have to cut back on many of the former Soviet commitments. One area it withdrew from was the Pacific rim; it gave up its naval base at Vladivostok. By chance, this coincided with the decision by the USA not to retain its naval base in the Philippines. Since Japan's fleet was negligible by international standards, this left China dominant over a large area of the western Pacific. It now chose to throw its weight about by claiming possession of the Spratly Islands, an area in the South China Seas that was believed to have large oil deposits. The islands had also been claimed variously by Indonesia, Malaysia, the Philippines and Vietnam. Ignoring these counter claims, China took the islands by force, sinking two Vietnamese vessels and frightening the other claimants off by sending nuclear-armed submarines to the area. Victory over the Vietnamese was particularly sweet for China, which had been harbouring resentment ever since its forces had been driven out of Vietnam in 1978 while trying to back Pol Pot's Cambodian invasion of that country.

The character of China's foreign policy

The manner of China's seizure of the Spratly Islands showed that, when it was in a position to be, the PRC could be as ruthless abroad as at home. This has become a defining characteristic of China's approach to foreign affairs. It is very much a matter of China first. It recognizes no international agreements that might damage its freedom to develop as it sees fit. A vivid example is its refusal to sign up to the Kyoto Protocol on control of pollution (discussed in Chapter 11). The reluctance of China to conform to international standards in relation to pollution is a feature of its approach to ethical issues generally. Compounding its own appalling record on human rights, is its willingness to develop relations with other authoritarian regimes, many of whom have been internationally condemned for the oppression of their peoples.

China in Africa

China is unworried by having to deal with Africa's dictators and warlords. It asks no questions about the political systems in the countries with which it is negotiating. The sensitivity that the West shows in such matters is not shared by the Chinese. Western governments and various international bodies, such as the World Bank, have threatened to withhold aid and trade from those regimes that will not make a commitment to democracy and human rights. China lays down no such requirements. When President Hu Jintao toured Africa in 2005–06, he made it clear that he did not come as a revolutionary or as a critic of any of the African governments. His sole declared aim was the furtherance of trade.

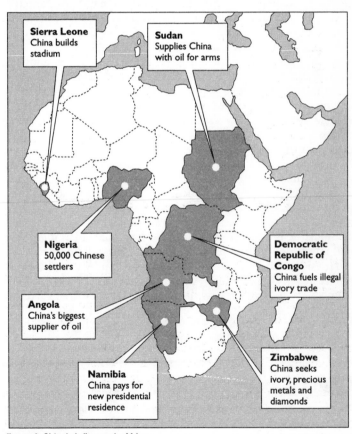

Sierra Leone
China builds stadium

Sudan
Supplies China with oil for arms

Nigeria
50,000 Chinese settlers

Democratic Republic of Congo
China fuels illegal ivory trade

Angola
China's biggest supplier of oil

Zimbabwe
China seeks ivory, precious metals and diamonds

Namibia
China pays for new presidential residence

figure 4 China's influence in Africa

The truth is China does not care. China's only concern is establishing its influence and expanding its commerce. Reflecting on his country's negotiations with China, the chief of the Nigerian Investment Commission commented: 'The USA will talk to you about governance, about efficiency, about security, about the environment. The Chinese just ask: "How do we procure the licence?".' Peter Takirambudde, the chief African representative of the organization Human Rights Watch put it in these terms: 'Wherever there are resources the Chinese are going to go there. They see no evil. They hear no evil. That's very bad for Africans.'

The result of such carefree attitudes is that China has expanded into Africa on an extraordinary scale. A great area of central Africa stretching from Sudan to Namibia has been targeted. Between 2003 and 2005 the turnover in trade between China and Africa rose from £22 million to £6.6 billion. China's chief economic aim in Africa is to get its hands on cheap raw materials: Chinese companies have lucrative contracts allowing them to extract oil, metal ores, diamonds and timber. China also provides aid and cheap loans as a way of establishing a strong commercial foothold. For some decades the large oil reserves in Angola attracted China's attention. That was why Chinese troops were to be found fighting in Angola's recent civil wars. Now Chinese soldiers have been replaced with Chinese money. As a result, Angola is currently China's largest overseas supplier of oil. In the early 2000s the PRC was quick to establish contacts in Sudan when it saw the difficulties the USA had got itself into in the region. China now supplies arms to Sudan in return for oil supplies. In Sierra Leone, Chinese workers are building the stadiums. It is Chinese workers who have built Namibia's new and lavish presidential palace, valued at £10 million. It has cost the president nothing; it has been given to him by the Chinese as a sweetener. One South African economist observed, 'The Chinese are getting away with claiming that they aren't like the other colonialists, but they are far more ruthless than the Brits ever were. If the British were our masters yesterday, the Chinese have come and taken their places.'

China's exploitative methods

Nor is it merely cash and trade in which China deals. There are few countries to be found in Africa now that do not ring to the sound of Chinese construction workers building railways, factories and tenements. This is because China insists on establishing a physical presence in Africa. As part of its commercial dealing, it has set up what are known as 'Baoding villages'. These are settlements where some 2,000 Chinese workers and advisers, together with their families, are located. By 2006, 28 of these had been established in various parts of Africa. So rapidly has the number of Chinese settlers in Nigeria grown, 60,000 by 2006, that a special news service has been set up to cater for them. To put this in perspective, it is worth pointing out that at no time during the period when Nigeria was a colony of Britain were there more than 40,000 British residents there.

One of China's advantages in seeking influence in Africa is that it presents itself as having a special historical link with Africa, claiming that from Mao onwards revolutionary China has been a beacon for the emergent nations struggling to throw off their colonial masters. It is certainly the case that the PRC sent economic and military assistance to a number of African countries during the Cold War, its principal aim having been not merely to make trouble for the West, but also to displace the Soviet Union as the leader of the anti-imperialist world.

It is this that makes the Chinese attitude towards Africa bitterly ironic. In a reverse form of racism, the Chinese workers in Africa, whose forebears a century ago were regarded as 'coolies', now look upon the African workers as inferiors. A Zimbabwean engineer in one of the copper mines said despondently that the Chinese 'despise blacks'. This is evident in the way Chinese companies based in Zimbabwe treat the local workers. Slave wages, denial of employee rights, and frequent accidents caused by lack of maintenance are the norm. The same Zimbabwean commented ruefully that this situation was hardly surprising since 'after all, that's how they run things at home'. The abused workers can expect no help from their own government; Robert Mugabe's regime with its 'look East' policy is not prepared to take up their case at the risk of upsetting Zimbabwe's Chinese paymasters. It was the Chinese who gave Mugabe £7 million to pay for the special tiles on the wall of his official residence in Harare. It is also Chinese poachers who are responsible for the largest number of thefts of ivory from Zimbabwe's game reserves, which for obvious reasons the government takes no serious steps to prevent. The Chinese have also been revealed as the main buyers of ivory in the Democratic Republic of the Congo. Without their involvement this internationally outlawed trade would collapse.

China's displacing of the West in Africa

China's inroads into Africa pose a great difficulty for the Western world. For all its good intentions, the West is losing the battle to bring Africa to its way of thinking about how people should be treated and how economic growth should be planned. G8 summits, debt cancellation, and Live-Aid concerts are all very well; they denote a genuine wish of Western governments and people to relieve the impoverishment of Africa. But they are unrealistic. A point on which most Africa-helpers agree is that the continent is in need of good governance; until African governments begin to make the people's needs a priority, rather than their own selfish ends, poverty and misery will remain. However, persuading governments to see it in that same way is the problem. China has been pouring millions of dollars in gifts and low-interest loans into the coffers of the corrupt African regimes. It is little wonder that those regimes regard Western entreaties with indifference or derision. They have no reason to listen. It is all a matter of hard economics. Notions of liberty have no influence in such a context. Regimes get their funds, and lots of them, from China. This has destroyed the West's ability to offer incentives to Africa's leaders that might make them better disposed towards introducing democracy. This point was memorably put by *The Times* Africa correspondent. He wrote of the extraordinary situation in which the Western sympathizers with Africa have put themselves. They are trying 'to pressure China to pressure African leaders to allow themselves to be voted out of office'.

One absurd result of the dependence of Africa's corrupt regimes on China is that the quality of the goods that China sends to Africa is invariably sub-standard. For example, of the 50 buses that Zimbabwe bought from China in 2004, none is still useable. It is as if Africa is being used as a dumping ground for China's industrial rejects. Why is this tolerated? The explanation is that Africa's corrupt governments are little concerned over it. The money they receive directly and personally from China makes them willing to turn a blind eye to shoddy Chinese imports. It is the African people who suffer. As a consequence there is a deep sense of frustration among ordinary Africans. They know they are being cheated and they know their own governments are complicit in the fraud. As a professor at Harare University put it: 'The resentment towards the Chinese is not only widespread, it's deeply rooted.'

The damage to Africa

China's exploitation of Africa is threatening to have tragic consequences. Chinese policies are stifling Africa's chances of ending the poverty that besets it. The African continent's great problem has been that it is essentially a producer of raw materials. The whole of modern economic history shows that primary producers have always been at the mercy of the buyers who control the prices. Wealth is created by the turning of raw materials into manufactured goods. This involves industry and it is the industrial nations who have become rich and powerful. If African states are to cure their poverty they have to become manufacturing economies; they would then be able to compete on genuine terms in world markets. The West has acknowledged this and admitted that its own imperialist policies did too little to advance Africa's real economic interests. But now a new imperialism has taken hold. China's current economic invasion of Africa threatens the continent's chance of achieving modernization. China is tapping Africa as a source of raw materials, deliberately keeping it at the level of primary producer. A South African professor gave an example of how this happens. 'China is forcing Africa back into the role of raw material suppliers – undermining its textile industry and importing raw cotton instead.'

Chinese expansion elsewhere

It is not only in Africa that China has made its play. Various countries in South America have been promised the equivalent of 100 billion dollars in the decade from 2005–15 in return for their readiness to enter into commercial contracts with China. Again, no awkward ethical strings were attached to the agreements. Belatedly, the West has awoken to the threat that China represents in Africa and elsewhere. In 2006, the United States' government called for China to end its support for 'egregious violators of human rights' and appealed to it to abandon its 'unfair business practices'. Such pleas are unlikely to make much difference to China.

Insofar as it feels obliged to answer for its policies, it points out that when the Western powers were expanding uninvited into foreign countries, including China, they were prepared to make deals with any local or national leaders who were willing to serve their imperialist cause; human rights did not come into it then. The Chinese view of the West's attempts to lecture it about respecting political freedoms and behaving responsibly towards the environment is that they are all hypocritical, a matter of 'don't do as we do (or did), do as we say'. The Western powers were quite prepared in their heyday to corrupt the earth and enslave its peoples. Having made themselves rich by doing so, they have now developed a conscience and wish to prevent anyone else from growing rich in a similar way. This attitude, drawn from its deep sense of historical grievance, means that China views issues in a fundamentally different way from its international critics and would-be persuaders.

Chinese arms sales

The truth is the PRC will establish contact with any region where it thinks it might be able to assert an influence. Belarus in Eastern Europe is one example. It is not the immediate economic gains, though these, it hopes, will follow; it is the mere fact of spreading itself in the world. In the Middle East the PRC's basic approach is to find out what the American view is and then oppose it. Hence it was reluctant to join in any formal censure of Iran's moves towards building nuclear weapons. Moreover, evidence suggests that China has assisted Iran in developing its nuclear technology by supplying scientific and military information and selling equipment. It has certainly sold a great many conventional arms to Iran. China is now one of the world's leading arms sellers. Again, it asks no questions of the buyers about the uses to which the weapons might be put. Nepal, which bought 25,000 Chinese rifles and 18,000 grenades, Burma and Sudan are among its clients and it has been said that without Chinese arms, which included fighter planes and helicopters, the Sudanese government's suppression of the Darfur region in 2005–06 could not have been undertaken.

Pakistan has bought over a billion dollars' worth of military equipment from China as well as having been helped by China in developing its atomic weapons. In the civil wars in Eritrea and Ethiopia, China has supplied both sides with arms. China's response is that all the major powers sell arms on the international market and while some of the powers place embargoes on sales to some countries this is from political not humanitarian considerations. Furthermore, Beijing points out, China is a long way behind the USA, Britain and France in the export of weapons. There are also defenders of the PRC who suggest that arms dealing is not actively pursued by the government but is the work of private companies. The problem with that argument is that since arms dealers in China are under government control, any sales they make must reflect government approval if not actual policy.

China and North Korea

China was placed in an awkward position in July 2006 when its neighbour and fellow Communist state, North Korea, in the face of near universal censure, and in disregard of non-proliferation treaties that it had signed, test launched seven medium and long-range missiles capable of carrying nuclear warheads. That the firing was largely unsuccessful, with the missiles plopping rather tamely into the Sea of Japan, did not make it less of an international incident. China along with Russia were the only two major countries not to back a UN resolution formally condemning North Korea. Nonetheless, China had been irritated by Pyongyang's failure to heed its request to call off the launching. Ever since the Korean War in the early 1950s when the young PRC fought on North Korea's side and managed to hold the American-dominated UN army to a stalemate, China has regarded itself as a protector of its eastern neighbour. It invariably gave support to North Korea's successive dictators, Kim Il-sung and his son, Kim Jong-il. There was a Chinese saying that China was as close to North Korea as 'lips are to teeth'. China has certainly always been reluctant to criticise its Communist neighbour despite the dangerous nuclear posturing of Kim Jong-il, who has become more irresponsible the deeper his country slides into bankruptcy and poverty.

The United States at whom most of Kim's antics have been directed wanted international pressure applied to North Korea. In response to this, a six-nation forum was set up, its members being Japan, Russia, USA, North and South Korea with China as host nation and convenor. The aim was for the other parties to organize economic aid for North Korea in return for its cutting back on its nuclear weapons programme. But in September 2005, North Korea accused the others of bad faith and withdrew from the forum. This left Beijing in a difficult position. It did not want to appear to be doing Washington's bidding but it still wished to keep a controlling hand on North Korea. It hoped to do so by using informal channels through which to continue exerting its influence. That was why it felt aggrieved by Kim's going ahead with the tests in defiance of its advice. Nevertheless, in the diplomatic wrangling that followed the tests, the PRC said that it would not accept any UN resolution that included a reference to the possibility of force being used against North Korea; if such a resolution were tabled, China declared it would exercise its veto against it. At a G8 meeting in St Petersburg later in July 2006, tension had eased somewhat. The PRC's president, Hu Jintao, announced that the USA and China 'had agreed to move forward with the six-party talks so that the entire Korean peninsula can be denuclearized through negotiation'. Hu's words were applauded by Condoleezza Rice, the American Secretary of State, who regards the best way of limiting the North Korean threat to be for the USA and the PRC to act in unison.

However, her views are not shared by all American officials. There are influential voices in the White House and in the Pentagon that argue that 'honeying up' to China is not the best policy. It has not worked in the past, they say, which is the reason for the present Korean nuclear crisis, the Chinese having given considerable assistance to North Korea in the development of its nuclear programme. The argument runs that, if the USA tries to treat China as a partner in dealing with Korea, this will deflect attention from China's own arms build-up along the Pacific rim with its strongly implied threat to Taiwan.

The question that the USA often asks is why does China need such arms, since, with the Cold War long over, it is not internationally threatened. The answer from a Chinese perspective is that all great powers, the USA for example, believe in their right to strengthen themselves by all legitimate means. It is an aspect of great power status. It is significant that the PRC has frequently used its veto in the UN Security Council to block various American and Western initiatives regarding peace plans in the world's trouble spots. This may have little to do with the merits of the specific issue or the particular proposals. It may be much more to do with China's wish to assert itself on the world stage and increase its influence in key areas. Whatever the rights and wrongs of such arguments, it is apparent than China's future relations with North Korea and, indeed, with the USA has become one of the major international questions of the age.

This was dramatically emphasized early in October 2006, when North Korea detonated what appeared to be an atomic device.

If this was indeed the case, then Asia's pariah nation was now a nuclear power. Beijing declared itself 'outraged' that Kim Jong Il, after all that had gone before, should do this without consulting the PRC, its neighbour and protector. Nevertheless, when Condoleezza Rice immediately went on a series of lightning visits to Japan, South Korea, Russia and the PRC to persuade all those regional powers to back a UN resolution imposing tough sanctions on North Korea, China hung back. It was willing to support some measures but declared that these must not be so punitive as to push Kim Jong Il into a desperate act. China's anxieties were very understandable. It did not wish to destroy what remained of its special diplomatic links with North Korea. More significant still, it was only too aware that if the worst happened and North Korea lashed out in wild nuclear abandon then the fall out, in its figurative and its deadly literal sense, might well come China's way.

China and India

In its early years, the PRC's relations with its Himalayan neighbour had been very cordial. Both nations had recently emerged from the shadow of foreign domination; the gaining of Indian independence in 1947 and the formation of the PRC in 1949 were momentous achievements. The two countries seemed to have much in common. Yet Sino-Indian relations have been subject to constant strain. India had responded with alarm when China took over Tibet in 1950. The line between Tibet and India had been drawn by Britain in 1913, an arbitrary boundary that the Chinese had never accepted. Sino-Indian border clashes continued throughout the 1950s as the PLA, extending its control over Tibet, pushed into Indian territory. Tensions became tauter still in 1959 when Nehru's government, in the face of angry protests from Beijing, granted sanctuary in Sikkim to the Dalai Lama. A full-scale Sino-Indian war eventually broke out in 1962 along the Himalayan border. The Indian forces came off worse in the bitter conditions. A formal peace was negotiated but for decades the Tibetan issue and the disputed borders question remained unresolved and divisive.

However, in July 2006, the Chinese government took a big step towards repairing its relations with India. The ceremonial opening of the Silk road through the Himalayas at the Nathun–La pass, which had been closed in 1962 by India to prevent Chinese troops crossing, marked a new departure. The trading agreement between India and the PRC, which accompanied the symbolic opening of the mountain pass is of little moment in itself, but it does represent China's determination to improve its relations with the countries on its western borders where its most troublesome independence movements are to be found. Since the war in 1962 China, to the anger of the Indians, had treated the border state of Sikkim as if it were an independent nation rather than part of India. As part of the improvement in Sino-Indian relations that the July 2006 accord represented, China agreed to recognize Sikkim as belonging to India.

Not everyone reacted to the July events with enthusiasm. The separatists, for example, in Tibet and Xinjiang who want to loosen Beijing's grip over them, interpreted China's agreement with India not as diplomatic goodwill but as a means by which China could apply even tighter control over its western border provinces and so suppress the independence movements. Tibetan nationalist sympathizers fear that the opening of the Nathun–La pass will make it easier for China to pursue Tibetan dissidents across the border and threaten the Dalai Lama who has his exiled base in Sikkim. Sceptical Indians are also concerned about China's deeper intentions. They worry that Chinese spies will infiltrate Sikkim in search of military secrets. There are Indian politicians and military leaders who warn of 'encirclement' by China. They mean by this that the Chinese, in addition to turning Tibet into the strongest armed province in the country, have made efforts to establish agreements with a whole range of nations that could be said to ring India geographically. Among these are Burma, Sri Lanka, Bangladesh and Nepal, the last named being the area from where the Naxalites, a guerrilla movement claiming to be inspired by Mao Zedong's revolutionary ideas, have launched terrorist attacks on Indian targets. But the country that most excites Indian anxiety is Pakistan. Tensions between Hindu India and Muslim Pakistan have been tense for decades and both are now nuclear-armed. India feels it has good reason to be suspicious of any developments involving the Chinese that might threaten its security.

The current rivalry between China and India is understandable. It is not only about borders and security. It relates to the present and future status of the two countries as great economic powers.

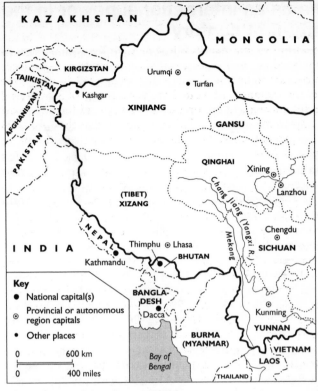

figure 5 China and its western neighbours

At the moment, China is far stronger economically than India. Its GDP in 2005 was £1.25 trillion compared with India's £443 billion and its surplus trade balance £120 billion against India's deficit of £30 billion. However, some statisticians forecast that in a matter of decades India's population will have overtaken China's 1.3 billion and India will thus be poised to become China's major challenger and competitor in international trade and commerce. Further predictions suggest that by the middle of the twenty-first century India will have caught up and joined China and the USA as the three dominant industrial nations in the world. Of course, none of this is certain. It may be that neither China nor India will fulfil the expectations. All manner of developments and crises could intervene. But the potential is there.

China as an international power in the twenty-first century

Communism remains the justification for the continued rule of the CCP in China. But the key factor about China today is not that it is a Communist power, but that it is a super power. Ever since it was subjected to foreign domination in the nineteenth century it has been China's aim to recover its national greatness. All the revolutionary parties in China had this basic purpose. It was what inspired Mao Zedong in his massive restructuring of the nation, it was the fundamental reason for Deng Xiaoping's new era modernizations, and it continues to shape the policies of the present Chinese government. China wishes to develop itself as a powerful nation not in order to further world revolution but simply to assert itself on the world stage. In that sense, China is a rogue state. It is seldom easy to anticipate what its response will be in any given situation. The PRC does not really have a foreign policy; it reacts to events as it sees fit at the time. It has inherited from the Cold War years a historical antipathy to the USA and the West, which means that it tends to take the side of the USA's opponents. But this policy is not set in stone; it can be co-operative when it chooses to be, as its trade relations show.

China's only criterion for action is whether it can derive some form of advantage for itself. Its place on the Security Council of the UN, a position denied it for so long, gives it the opportunity to exercise its veto over crucial UN resolutions. It did this over the Bosnian question in the late 1990s and over the Middle East in the early 2000s. Too often, according to exasperated UN diplomats, China shows a whimsical approach, judging issues not on their merits but by what opportunities they provide for China to make mischief. Perhaps it relates back to the 1970s, and even earlier, when China was debarred from what it regarded as its proper place in the councils of the world.

09

tensions within changing China – politics and culture

This chapter will cover:
- China's politics
- the threats to traditional culture
- old habits, new ways
- the media explosion.

The political system in China

Figure 6 indicates how the Communist Party's power supposedly derives from the people. The party's assertion is that all the blocks represent the inter-related power sources, each performing a particular function, but all drawing their authority from the CCP which is the ultimate expression of the people's will.

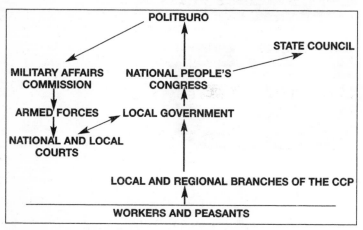

figure 6 the Chinese Communist Party

As shown in figure 7, the PRC's government in Beijing administers China through six regional bureaux.

The system is not as smoothly linked as it looks on paper. The basic point is that whatever the appearances, the CCP rules. Its authority is unchallengeable, since it is based on 'democratic centralism'. This is the notion developed by Lenin in Soviet Russia and taken up by Mao Zedong in China that the only proper form of government in a truly socialist state is one where the people obey the government. This is not tyranny but its very opposite. The argument is that while 'the people', 'the masses', are the source of true authority, they are represented by the Chinese Communist Party, which governs in their name and with their interests paramount. That is why there is no need for any other party; it would make no sense to have an opposition to the party of the people. The government and people are one. But why not, then, simply allow the people to govern directly? The answer is a practical one; in a country the size of China it would be impossible for direct democracy to work; the will of 1.3 billion people has to be channelled. The CCP is the channel. The insight and wisdom of the party's leaders enables them to interpret the people's wishes.

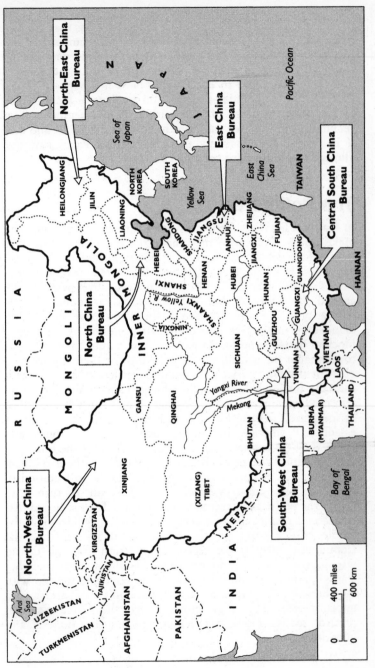

figure 7 the administrative divisions within the PRC

The Chinese Communist government makes much of its claim to be a true democracy by pointing to the elections that are held in the regions and in the villages. What the government does not emphasize is that no party, other than the CCP, may put up candidates. Perhaps with the odd exception of an independent who in any case has to declare that he is not opposed to the CCP, the list of candidates to serve on a village or local council is composed entirely of Communist Party members. It is reminiscent of the 'free' elections held in Stalin's USSR and is as if in British elections only the Conservative Party, say, was allowed to put forward candidates.

The Politburo

In reality, China is governed by some nine or ten persons who make up the Politburo; they make the major decisions. The reason for such concentration of power is that official titles mean little in China. Deng Xiaoping dominated Chinese politics for 18 years after 1979 but held no executive position. He carried the honorary but vague title of Paramount Leader. Authority in China is exercised by those who have managed to manoeuvre themselves into dominant positions by building a block of party supporters large enough in number and influence to outmatch other challengers. In return for their loyalty they are provided with perks, pensions and privileges. None of this is formally acknowledged, but the Chinese Communist Party is, in effect, a huge dispenser of patronage. It may fairly be described as organized corruption. In such a system, conformity is essential. Promotion and success depend less on ability and talent than on connections. It is very rarely that there is open dispute within the party. Rivalries abound but these result in infighting not in open confrontation. There is no tradition of legitimate opposition or protest. To speak out of turn is to offend the political correctness that prevails. The essence of that correctness is unswerving acceptance of the party line. Since the whole edifice rests on the fundamental notion that the Communist Party is the repository of truth and can do no wrong, there can be no criticism. Should a party member transgress not only does he lose all the privileges that go with membership; he faces a strong possibility of arrest and imprisonment. The tragic truth is that the Chinese system rewards toadying and sycophancy and punishes honesty and integrity.

The character of the present Chinese Communist Party

It is not political belief that sustains the CCP so much as the simple fact that it provides jobs for the boys. It has become a self-perpetuating establishment. History suggests that absolute systems are in the greatest danger when they begin to doubt themselves and try to reform. The signs are that the Chinese Communists took a very serious lesson from the dissolution of the USSR. There in the 1990s an apparently monolithic, unbreakable system crumbled when it admitted it had made mistakes and tried to rectify these. The admission by the Communist Party of the Soviet Union that it had made errors destroyed its credibility and it fell apart. What hastened its end were its economic bankruptcy and its previous failure to suppress the separatist movements with the Eastern bloc and within the USSR itself. On both those points China has a strength and determination that the Soviet Union lacked. It has a booming economy and a determination to do whatever is necessary to suppress the forces of Chinese separatism. The government will not tolerate secession in the troubled western provinces. There is no evidence that the government has begun either to question its own infallibility or to lose the will to crush opposition. The CCP continues to spread its net wide. In the universities, every faculty and department has a party commissar in residence who sits in at all the decision-making meetings and reports back to headquarters. Copy in newspapers has to be submitted to a party censor before publication.

Nevertheless, the CCP has shown realism in not relying on repression alone. Aware that the great economic strides China was making had produced a new class of wealthy entrepreneurs, the CCP decided to bring them into the party, rather than risk their becoming a potentially dangerous force of opposition. In 2002, in a shrewd, calculated move, Jiang Zemin, who had just stepped down as President, persuaded the party to change its constitution. Membership was now to be open not only to workers and peasants but also to 'advanced social productive forces', in other words, China's new rich, the private money-makers who were building China's economy. It was an extraordinary accommodation for a revolutionary party to make. But it appeared to work. Within six weeks over 100,000 entrepreneurs had accepted the invitation to join the Chinese Communist Party. China's capitalists were now part of the political establishment.

The struggle between the traditional and the new

The omens are not good for those who would like to see traditional Chinese values survive. Whenever they are in open competition with Western values they lose out. Take the example of popular culture. The young of China have little interest in preserving the music, clothing and manners of traditional China. They thirst after Western pop music; rock bands proliferate; fashions are modelled on Western, which is to say primarily American, tastes. Coffee, which never seemed to suit the Chinese taste buds, is now drunk as a mark of sophistication by the yuppies of Beijing and Shanghai. The Western companies, Costa Coffee and Starbucks, have specifically targeted this group. In the words of Costa's chief, 'We're pioneering a fashionable lifestyle here. Anything Western catches on.' Chinese caterers now send their employees on courses abroad to learn how to make coffee western style. The very existence of yuppies in China's cities shows how far the nation's progressive young people have accepted that the Western lifestyle is the one to emulate.

McDonald's, whose logo is as distinctive a sign of Western capitalism as the Coca-Cola bottle, already has 750 outlets spread around China's cities and plans to open another hundred in time for the Olympics in 2008. The head of 'McDonald's China' announced plans for linking up with Sinopec, the company that runs most of China's petrol stations, with a view to introducing the Chinese to the idea of the drive-through. He declared enthusiastically, 'We see the future of China with cars, communities and houses spreading out. We think the potential for drive-throughs is huge.' A Chinese name has already been chosen for them, *De Lai Su*, which means 'Come and get it – fast.'

Learning English has become a craze and an industry. Quite apart from its commercial benefits, English is regarded as a 'must' language for those who want to be truly modern. English Language schools have mushroomed and English-speaking visitors are sought out and engaged in conversation by eager young people keen to show off their command of English. The yobbery and anti-social behaviour which has accompanied the growing affluence of the West has begun to spread in China. Ill-behaved and foul-mouthed youths have become a problem on the streets of China's cities. Appeals to them to remember that they are giving Communism a bad name have little effect, so the authorities have tried emphasizing Confucian values of harmony and ordered behaviour. But it seems the Chinese are engaged in an ironic trade-off. They flood the international markets with their manufactured goods while the West floods China with its sub-culture. As with money, so with manners, the bad drives out the good.

Rich and poor

Money provides an interesting insight into modern China and its attitudes. Two-thirds of the Chinese population, the great bulk of them living in the countryside, have a disposable income of about £1 a day. They tend to be despised by the moneyed classes in the cities. But even among these there is great diversity. This inequality is fascinatingly illustrated in the current Chinese practice of queuing. It is hard to find evidence of the Communist principle of social equality in action. As people acquire more money banks become increasingly crowded. With all the technological gains China has made, its people are reluctant to engage in online banking or use credit and debit cards. There are cash dispensers but most Chinese still prefer to draw their money and pay their bills in person in a bank. This has led to a surge in bank business and ever-lengthening queues. Bank customers with more than 300,000 yuan (£20,000) in their accounts do not have to queue; they have separate teller's windows reserved for them which they go straight up to. The rest with smaller accounts have to queue, often for hours. But there is a way round it. Banks have taken to providing machines from which numbered tickets are drawn; the intention, as at many British supermarket counters, is to create a first-come, first-served system. However, enterprising youngsters have developed a system in which they arrive early, take handfuls of tickets, or buy them from existing queuers, and then sell them on for 50 yuan or so to those eager to jump the queue. In such circumstances, customary Chinese restraint often breaks down and near riots ensue. Police have been called out to several banks in Beijing.

It is difficult to see how traditional culture can survive as a mainstream activity in modern China. It was, after all, the product of a contemplative age which has largely gone. It has been superseded by a global, Americanized, popular culture that the young in China, as in most countries, find so attractive. This readiness of a traditional society to abandon its tradition is not so puzzling when it is remembered how willingly and violently China's young, on a word from Mao, set about destroying the four olds on which Chinese civilization rested.

But, perhaps, it is not all bad news on the cultural front. The great canon of Western classical music, which was outlawed in Mao's time, is now performed by Chinese orchestras and soloists of the highest international renown. This is a fascinating restoration. Since the nineteenth century, musicologists, Asian as well as Western, have accepted that traditional Chinese music lacked depth. Written in a rigidly formalized style, it was essentially diversionary music and not meant to be listened to as something of intrinsic worth. That was why the Chinese very quickly took up Western music when it entered China; its profundity and emotional range made it hugely appealing.

People on bicycles?

The humble bicycle is a striking example of changing China. Until very recently the bicycle was king in the nation's towns and cities. In Beijing there were official government cars, taxis and public transport vehicles, but the great mass of the people rode bikes. The roads were filled with them. It was the first thing visitors noticed. Every Beijing resident seemed to travel by cycle. Most rode the single geared 'Flying pigeon', a sturdy black machine with upright handlebars, front basket and rear panniers. The bikes took their name from the state-owned cycle company that began to mass produce them in 1949, the year the Communists came to power. The cycles did not merely carry the rider. It seemed to the casual visitor that every other bike was loaded with crates of fruit and vegetables or cages of chickens and ducks or pigs. Indeed, it was a common belief that the cross-bar was specially strengthened so as to be able to carry pigs slung beneath. The boxes and cages were stacked in storeys so high that the rider's rearward vision was totally obscured. There were thrills and spills and collisions but these were rarely serious.

However, these quaint scenes are rapidly becoming a thing of the past. Until the late 1990s, 4 million flying pigeons were sold annually, but that number has plummeted. The figure for 2005 was one and a half million and of these one-third were sold abroad. The special cycle lanes on the major roads in Beijing no longer exist and in some areas cycles are forbidden altogether. The dwindling number of riders now have to dice with death as they compete for space with the ever-growing number of cars that now choke the city's roads. Around 1,500 new cars are added to the capital's streets every day. By 2006 there were 50,000 miles of three-lane motorway being built in China. One Chinese oil company, Sinopec, alone owns 30,000 petrol stations in China and intends to open a further 500 annually. In an incident that seemed sadly symbolic of the new Beijing, Weng Fenghe vowed never to ride a bike again after been knocked over and seriously injured. Weng was chairman of the Chinese Bicycle Association.

The pedestrian fares little better. To the risk of being knocked down by motorists, whose standards of driving beggar description, is added the prospect of his falling foul of the State. In Shanghai, China's most densely populated city, the authorities have adopted tight measures to control the situation. On-the-spot fines of Y50 (£3) are imposed on anyone who dares cross at anything other than controlled pedestrian lights. The same fine is imposed on those foolish enough to step off the kerb before or after the light is green. Nor is being caught the lottery that it is in many countries. The Chinese town dweller is the most photographed and filmed person on earth. Cameras are everywhere. Moreover, for jaywalkers, fines are only the start of their problems. It is the practice in Shanghai for films of the miscreants to be sent to the factories, shops or offices where they work. The incriminating videos are then screened for everyone to see. To add to their woes, the guilty ones find that their pay packets have been docked to cover the cost of the fine just in case they are slow to pay. If such measures still fail to bring the sinners to mend their ways, they are likely to suffer the ultimate indignity of being turned into celebrities; their deeds will be shown on public-broadcast television and enlarged pictures of their faces will appear on giant billboards.

The word sinners was not used loosely in the last sentence. The aim of the authorities is to characterize traffic and jaywalking offences not as minor crimes but as moral failings. It is part of that long-standing tradition in China of publicly humiliating the wrong-doer. Among the Chinese the fear of losing face or being ridiculed in public has always been a powerful check on social behaviour. It was what made the self-criticism sessions such an effective instrument of control in Mao's China. The essence of this moral approach is contained in the title of the body responsible for tackling China's traffic problems, 'The Spiritual Civilization Office', which claims in good Confucian style that its aim is to create 'harmony' on the streets.

But modern ways have intervened. China's urban young are not as willing as their forebears to be patronized. Early in 2006, a young woman refused to pay an on-the-spot fine imposed by Traffic Assistant Tong, one of five smartly uniformed guardians of a single crossing point in Shanghai's Huaihai Road, an upmarket shopping area. When Traffic Assistant Tong continued to demand payment the woman flew at him, hitting him over the head with her bag and scratching his face. For this outbreak of pedestrian rage, she was imprisoned for ten days and her fine was increased. In reporting the case, the newspapers took gloating delight in recording that the young woman had gained a post-graduate degree at a British university.

The treatment of animals

There were two features of China's ways of doing things that Western visitors tended to find offensive. One was the Chinese habit of spitting in public; Western tolerance was tested by the sound and sight of people voiding their rheum and the puddles of mucous and saliva it created. The other was the Chinese treatment of animals. There are not many cats and dogs to be seen loose in China's towns and cities. That is because the Chinese eat them. In certain regions cat or dog is regarded as a great delicacy. But the thought of what are domestic pampered pets in Europe and the USA being reared and eaten like a pig or chicken is unacceptable to many Western visitors. But all this may well change in the new China. Aware of the distress that these customs can cause, the authorities promoted an anti-spitting campaign urging the Chinese people not to expectorate in public places and to use a little thing called a handkerchief.

Animal rights is not a big movement in China but it is a growing one. In 2006, a group of 40 demonstrators picketed the Fangi Cat Meatball Restaurant in Shenzen in southern China. They carried banners proclaiming 'Cats and dogs are friends of humans. Stop eating them please.' The protest was enough to make the manager promise that cat dishes would be removed from the menu, which was quite a concession given that cat was the only food the restaurant served. Caged birds have long been kept as pets in China but not four-legged animals. This, despite Mao Zedong's attempt to destroy China's bird life during the Great Leap Forward. The attitude was essentially practical. Cats and dogs were seen as a source of food; there was little point in indulging them as pets. The new town-dwellers are beginning to keep cats and dogs as adornments to their new houses and apartments. If this becomes an established practice it will mark another divide between rural and urban China, a detail in itself, but an indication of changing cultural attitudes.

W.W.W.

The conflict between the old and the new in China's attempt to modernize economically, while at the same time prevent the development of political freedoms, is strikingly evident in the PRC's response to the world's most significant development in communications technology – the world wide web. Access to the net first became available in China in 1994. By 2006, there were over 100 million Chinese web users, which represented 10 per cent of the population and made China the second largest user after the USA. Projections suggest that the number could rise to over 750 million by 2010 – half China's population. Recognizing that this explosion in web use is the biggest threat to the absolutism of its Communist rule, the PRC government had made great efforts to restrict and censor it. The government has set up a 'firewall'; this is a system that scrambles those web pages that the authorities do not want the people to have access to. The obvious forbidden pages are those dealing with the themes that the government regard as either politically subversive – religion, democracy, Tibet, Taiwan, for example, or morally dubious – such as chat lines and pornography sites. In January 2006, Google, the California-based web company, won permission from the PRC to extend its services into China. The catch was that this was granted only on condition that Google would not provide any pages of which the Chinese authorities disapproved. There were cries in the West that for Google to make itself a party to censorship offended the basic principle of freedom of information. The criticism stung Google's executives; in June 2006 the company announced that it was reconsidering its position with a view to relinquishing its franchise.

A battle has ensued between the government and the web providers. Although the providers have developed ingenious coding techniques to dodge the restrictions, the government has countered this by using heavy-handed tactics. It holds all the IT companies in China responsible for what becomes available to users. Those providing prohibited material are reckoned to be as guilty as those searching for it. As a Western-trained Chinese IT expert put it after examining the situation in the PRC: 'The government makes every digital enterprise, online hosting service and commercial portal accountable for what they publish.' Another advantage for the authorities is that the majority of China's web users do not own their own computers. They use the internet cafés. This makes it easier for the government to exert control. In 2004 alone, over 45,000 net cafés were closed down for failing to satisfy government censors.

The PRC's campaign against web users contributes to its grim human rights record. Amnesty International yearly records the hundreds of Chinese who have been imprisoned for putting forbidden material online or downloading from it. 'Reporters Without Borders', a web-watcher organization in France, has described Beijing as 'the world champion of internet censorship'. In July 2006, Li Yuaniong, a reporter on a newspaper in the southern city of Bijie, received a two-year prison sentence for using foreign web sites to post criticisms of the government; his crime was defined as 'subversion'.

A number of the leading internet companies, including Yahoo and Microsoft, continue to operate in China. Human rights groups have attacked them for this. Yahoo was severely censured for allegedly passing on information that led to the arrest and imprisonment of a number of web users in Beijing. The problem illustrates the dilemma of all the countries and companies that trade with China. That country offers huge possibilities for investment, sales and profits. But the moral price is that they have to ignore China's human rights record. Some commercial companies feel justified in pointing out that as long as national governments continue to maintain full diplomatic relations with China, and, indeed, to do their utmost to expand their commerce there, it makes little sense for individual companies to take an ethical stance. Nor do ordinary citizens entirely escape the problem. As shoppers, do they buy or boycott those goods, marked 'Made in China' that fill the shops and supermarket shelves? In many instances the goods have been produced by exploited workers in sweat shops or in the slave-labour conditions of the laogai.

Up to the present the government has been winning its struggle. Its surveillance methods have proved more effective than the users' attempts to counter them. This is not surprising given that the large-scale spending on it by the government far outweighs that spent by the users. Yet whatever success the PRC has in restricting its people's access to the internet is double-edged. The government is faced with a dilemma. As its agreement with Google showed, it is aware that the internet is indispensable for China if it is to sustain its drive for economic progress; the demands of industrial production and international commerce make it so. China will have to make up its mind whether the internet is a friend or foe. There is also the argument that no matter how hard the Chinese government, or any government for that matter, might try to control the web, the technology will in the end defeat them.

The media

Control of the media remains a basic objective of the Communist government. Periodically, editors and journalists are dismissed or demoted on the order of the government. The official justification that invariably accompanies such interference with such freedoms is that the people need protection from misinformation and error.

There are nine state-owned Chinese daily newspapers, which present the CCP's line. These have a national circulation. In addition, each province and city have party-sponsored newspapers. Alongside these, in most provinces, there are private commercially owned newspapers. It is these that are particularly closely monitored by state censors. Most of them play safe by employing a form of self-censorship which means they avoid touching on sensitive political issues whose mention would incur the government's anger. Conventional journalism and the internet have exposed injustice and created debates in China about social issues, public health, pollution and civil rights. The government lets some investigative journalism flourish, then clamps down. Editors are fired, web sites blocked, newspapers closed, and journalists imprisoned.

Television is another area where the government intrudes. In total there are over 2,000 state-run or state-controlled TV channels, which are accessible in all but the remotest regions. One billion of China's 1.3 billion people watch television, which, as in most countries, has become the largest provider of news and popular entertainment. In addition to the state network, there is a growing number of pay-to-view channels. Foreign programmes are broadcast but these have first to be vetted by the State Administration for Radio, Film and Television, which acts as the largest state censor in China. Broadcasts that are held to be a danger to 'national security or political stability' are not passed for viewing. Producers often claim that this definition is too widely interpreted by the censors who act as a brake on artistic expression. But the concept of artistic freedom is alien to Chinese tradition and producers very seldom get their way in any dispute with the authorities.

The Beijing Olympics in 2008 will be a fascinating test of the PRC's ability to present itself to the world as a modern nation. It is true that Nazi Germany in 1936 successfully hid its authoritarianism and racism and made its hosting of the Olympics a great propaganda success. It will be interesting to see whether the PRC can do the same. Never before will it have been scrutinized so intensely by the international media.

10

corruption, sickness and poverty in China

This chapter will cover:
- the extent of corruption in China
- health problems
- the spread of poverty
- upheaval on the land.

'They are all on the fiddle'

In July 2005, draped on the wall of a half-constructed building in Shanghai, there was a long banner with large painted characters. It read: 'Do not trust any of the officials in this city. They are all on the fiddle.' The banner had been put up overnight and the police had it quickly removed in the morning. But by then it had made its point, one that everybody could recognize. It referred to a crisis that affects not only Shanghai but the whole of the nation; China is corrupt. It is so serious a problem that it might well destroy China's economic progress and bring down the Communist regime.

Arguably, one of the reasons why the Soviet Union collapsed so quickly in the early 1990s was that the communist system, despite its claim to represent the people, had become irredeemably corrupt. Its officials paid lip service to the collective principle but they lined their own pockets. Some observers suggest that China is heading in a similar direction. Behind the PRC's official commitment to the people's welfare lies a deeper cynicism. It is true the government every so often mounts well-publicized crackdowns on corruption and punishes the wrongdoers. But these are gestures, intended to blind the nation to the true scale of the problem.

A vivid example of the blight is to be seen in the planning for China's great flagship enterprise, the hosting of the 2008 Olympics. Beijing's dash to be ready for the event created a dream time for embezzlers. This is not surprising, given that the equivalent of £20 billion had been allocated by the government to the city (five times the amount earmarked for the London Olympics in 2012). In June 2006, President Hu Jintao was so embarrassed by charges that senior officials were on the take that he assumed personal control of the investigations. This led to the suspension of the director in charge of constructing the new stadiums and came on top of the dismissal of the deputy mayor of Beijing, Liu Zhihua, for having taken bribes from developers. When the case came to light, Liu was not helped by the revelation that he had installed a series of mistresses in his government-provided villa. One of the companies most implicated in corruption scandals was Capital Land, whose properties were so extensive that its chairman was nicknamed 'Beijing's landlord'. The fact that Capital Land was jointly owned by private shareholders and the Beijing City Council indicated how easily the public interest could be subordinated to private concerns. Too much money stuck to too many fingers.

Health

Graft infects everything – not simply politics and government, but education, welfare and health provision, the institutions on which ordinary Chinese depend. With the growth of corruption has come a decline in the idea of selfless public service. The people are being cheated by those who are supposed to protect them. One of the better features of the Mao years was that most Chinese had access to free medical treatment. GPs, known colloquially as 'the barefoot doctors', went around rural China providing treatment free of charge. Dr Liu Quan, who was one of these, recalled, 'In Chairman Mao's time, you could see a doctor whether you had money or not. We would carry out disease prevention, like injections.' Such a service no longer operates. There are no more barefoot doctors. A study by the World Health Organization (WHO) in 2005, comparing the quality of health care that various countries provided, ranked China 187th in a list of 191. The government claims that it does not have the resources to provide a full national health service for a billion and a quarter people. As Dr Hu Weimin, a heart specialist, commented: 'Our hospital's state funding isn't enough to even cover staff salaries for one month. Under the current system hospitals have to chase profits to survive.'

The result is that only those with money can be sure of receiving primary care and hospital treatment. Unsurprisingly, widespread corruption has crept into this vital area of Chinese life also. Knowing they are in a sellers' market, doctors are able to demand the highest rates for their services. They prescribe unnecessary treatments and drugs to boost their income. In one case, a girl with appendicitis had to go through over 100 separate tests including one for AIDS. The government's own statistics for the period 2000–03 revealed that while the number of patients treated in hospital dropped by 6 per cent hospital profits rose by over 70 per cent. One patient, Xie Pei, who was paying for her mother's treatment, has described what this means for ordinary Chinese: 'My friend was visiting me and a doctor asked her what my financial circumstances were like and what model of car I drove. The next day the doctor said the cost of the operation had gone up by £3,000.' The payments did not end there. The doctors demanded backhanders that did not go through the books: 'I gave £600 to the professor. Before the operation, a doctor told me that surgery would take place that night and I had to give money to others, including the anaesthetist. In the end I gave £1,000 in red packets.' The tragedy of this particular case is that the operation went wrong and the mother was left permanently paralysed.

Of course, there are still honest doctors in China, but where they have spoken out against the corruption they have often been threatened and on occasion physically attacked. One example is Dr Hu Weimin, the cardiologist quoted above. When he exposed his hospital's practice of overcharging and giving bogus diagnoses and treatment, he was assaulted and his family forced to move home for safety's sake.

AIDS in China

There is a dispute over whether there is an AIDS epidemic in China. Not surprisingly, the government denies there is one. In 2005, it quoted a figure of 650,000 recorded cases, adding that this compared with the figure for the previous year of 700,000. WHO observers say these figures are inaccurate, since they refer only to officially recorded cases in urban areas. Estimates suggest that the true figure, which would include rural China, is probably nearer a million and a half. While this still may not seem especially large in an overall Chinese population of 1.3 billion, the critical element is the rate of increase. The calculation is that at the current rate, China within a decade could have as many as 20 million AIDS cases. This would be an epidemic. A major problem in combating the spread is the poverty in rural areas, which, as in Africa, is where the disease tends to take a tenacious grip. This, together with the common boast among Chinese men that their favourite hobby is having sex, makes it difficult to control the disease in its most contagious areas. Condoms are of limited effectiveness since, quite apart from the strong prejudice against their use in rural China, sexual relations are the cause of only 20 per cent of AIDS cases. The main reason for the spread of the disease is contaminated blood from unscreened donors.

In 2003, the government introduced a 'four frees and one care' policy. This aimed to provide free drugs for HIV-infected addicts, pregnant women with HIV, and free care and education for the orphaned children of AIDS victims. China's prostitutes, whose number is estimated at between five to six million, have been targeted in government campaigns aimed at improving the knowledge and practice of safe sex. The campaigns have not always been well thought through. One difficulty is that since prostitution for 'commercial gain' is illegal in China, its practitioners are understandably reluctant to attend counselling and advice centres. There is also the notion among Chinese police forces that if a woman is found to have three or more condoms in her handbag this is sure proof she is a prostitute and so must be arrested.

Matters are not helped by the government's harrying of those who attempt to publicize the extent of AIDS. Newspapers have been shut down and their editors imprisoned or 'rectified', as the official jargon has it, for giving details. One editor received an eight-year sentence for writing about the Severe Acute Respiratory Syndrome (SARS) epidemic in China.

Poverty in China

China for centuries has had a shortage of land. Despite its vast size, it has comparatively little land suitable for farming and its climate renders large areas unproductive. In its broad geography, China is made up of a series of urban areas, located on the east coast and the main rivers, visibly and excitingly engaged in advancing the nation's march to capitalism. Behind these, stretching westwards, is a vast hinterland of poverty.

China might well be described as two nations – urban China and rural China. There is a huge disparity between town and country. The nation's growing wealth remains restricted to the cities. Rural China suffers acute poverty; many of its agricultural workers have a miserable existence. Indeed, China has some of the worst pockets of poverty in the world. The urban Chinese tend to look down upon their country cousins, regarding them as second class citizens. 'Country people are of the lowest quality', is typical of the comments made by town-dwellers who now say the word 'peasant' or 'farmer' with a sneer or a mocking laugh. It is akin to a form of racism.

The West is familiar with the images of wealthy Chinese in the cities, of discoing young people aping their western counterparts in their love of pop music and modern fashions, and of massive building projects that are changing the skyline of China at an extraordinary pace. What is not so often seen is the grimness of the conditions in which the rural population, still numbering some 700 million people, live. The gap between rich and poor continues to grow. This has been reflected in a great migration from the land to the towns and cities. In the last 30 years, around 150 million people have left the countryside.

Calculations indicate that a further 200 million will leave by 2040. The migrants come in desperate search for jobs and are willing to work for very low rates of pay. While not acknowledging it, the government and employers are quite happy with this, since it lowers overheads and allows China to keep the prices of its manufactured goods below those of its international competitors. This is why every other item picked up in stores and shops in the West seems to read 'Made in China'.

The plight of the rural migrants can be witnessed at many of the forecourts of the major railway stations in cities such as Beijing or Shanghai. Without accommodation and with no job obtained as yet, they line up in neat rows in disciplined Chinese fashion with their few possessions beside them. There they patiently wait, often for days, slowly changing places until they reach the front of the line. Here they are in a position to be spotted and chosen by the foremen who daily turn up in lorries to offer jobs at minimum rates, pick their workers from among the eager volunteers, and then ferry them to the building sites and factories. The opportunities for exploitation are many. Foremen pick those migrants who have paid them up front or are willing to pledge part of their meagre pay once they have started working. It is a scene redolent of Dickensian London where casual labourers fought at the dock gates to be selected by corrupt gang foremen for work unloading the ships.

Revolution in the countryside

Until recently, successive Chinese governments did little to address the problem of rural deprivation. Despite many public pronouncements to the contrary, the PRC put little investment into the land. Beginning with Mao, China's leaders saw the future in terms of industrial growth. The interests of those who lived on the land came a very poor second in the building of the new China. This has now belatedly and dramatically changed. The PRC now realizes that the land can no longer be ignored. This is far more than a question of economics; it is the political dangers that have pushed the government into action.

China's ruling Communist Party fears that if it cannot bring employment and growth to hinterland China, it will become increasingly difficult to maintain its control. It has come up with two answers to ensure its survival. The first is stopping the flood of peasants into the towns and cities that have reached saturation point. The second is to turn great swathes of the countryside into towns. Hence the massive building projects that have begun in many parts of rural China. Bulldozers raze the wooden houses, shacks and shops of what was once a village, and the land is pounded flat. They then rise on it concrete tenement blocks to house the displaced peasants. It is a breathtaking concept. As a piece of social engineering it ranks with Mao's enforced collectivization of the peasants in the 1950s.

Those who resist these changes and try to cling on to the traditional agricultural ways find themselves ignored or bypassed. Old-style farming and the way of life that went with it have no future. The task of the local Communist Party secretaries consists essentially of telling the peasants either to leave the land or stay and help build, and so become part of the new towns. There are no plans to preserve China's rural heritage. Modernity is everything.

For some all this has brought a tragic upheaval in their lives. They are the often uncomprehending victims of national policies decided thousands of miles away in a remote capital. For them it was never a matter of consultation. They were simply told what was going to happen. Occasionally the government called meetings that were supposedly an opportunity for local people to voice their concerns. But this was a charade. Complaints from the people were never going to be acted upon. Even in democratic countries it is very difficult for local people to reject a policy already decided on by central government. In China it is impossible. The will of the government has the force of holy writ. The role of the local Communist Party secretaries is critical in this respect. In theory, the secretary is the official who conveys the wishes of the local communities up the chain of command to the provincial and national party bosses who then act upon those wishes. But theory is all it is. In practice, the secretaries' task is to impose government and party decisions on the localities. There are secretaries who do genuinely work to help the community. Some are idealistic men or women who try to solve the everyday problems of their people by organizing improvements in such things as schooling and health care.

One such is Zhang Qiao, who has served as party secretary for over 20 years in Wuzhi, a small town in central China. Zhang understands his people and is genuinely distressed at their plight as their town is demolished around them. So far 43 families have accepted the inevitable and left. Zhang's job is to persuade the remaining five families to do the same. He knows they will have to go in the end but he wants to avoid using force to evict them. 'It is very sad. I have been on this land for decades, on the same fields as my ancestors, but I have to follow the party's direction and this is an important project and we should support it.' Zhang genuinely believes that the new towns will give the peasants far more than they could ever have got from their traditionally backbreaking 'face to the earth, back to the sky' work in the paddy fields. He is sure that once the villagers have come to see it in that light they will realize they are being liberated. But Zhang also knows just how big the change in their life has been and how bewildered these traditionally conservative people are by the sheer speed and scale of the changes around them. It is particularly difficult for the old who find it almost impossible to adapt to the new way of living forced upon them. One of the villagers who had been a farm manager asked Zhang how the party could seriously tell him to give up farming and take up one of the new jobs that the rebuilt area now offered. 'I am in my sixties – I don't know how to run a town business. How can I learn now?'

One of the major complaints put to Zhang Qiao by his villagers is one that is voiced frequently by China's peasants; they have not been dealt with fairly. The strongest grievance is over the compensation the peasants receive. In Wuzhi, after the farm land had been compulsorily purchased, the government reclassified it as land for commercial and business use and sold it to developers at 30 times the value of the compensation paid to the farmers. Sadly for the cheated peasants, most party secretaries are not like Zhang. They are not local to the community they serve; they are appointees sent from afar. Fundamentally their job is a political one, to keep things under control and prevent serious opposition to the party developing. Too often, secretaries simply become snoopers and informers, regarding themselves as enlightened beings whose job it is to bring the benefits of party wisdom to an ignorant people. Resentment against their interfering and patronizing ways is frequently strong but seldom voiced since it does not pay to fall foul of an official with such influence and authority. Nevertheless, in many rural areas the frustrations of farmers and villagers have led to organized protests, sometimes descending into riots. In 2004, there were over 70,000 public demonstrations.

Yet, in spite of the upheaval, the corruption and the unrest, there are some, perhaps a sizeable minority in Wuzhi and in other parts of China, who have welcomed the changes. After the initial disruption, they have come to appreciate the better housing and amenities they now enjoy. One bewildered peasant described his new way of life as being like 'a beggar living in a mansion'. The biggest gain has been in job prospects. Regularly paid employment contrasts very favourably with the seasonal uncertainties of peasant farming. As another villager put it to Zhang: 'Farming means a subsistence lifestyle, but the government is developing the place. The farmers don't realize how lucky they are. This is an opportunity that only comes once in a thousand years.'

But whatever the hopes that have been raised by the economic changes in China, a dark cloud hangs over China's poorest people. Poverty is at its worst among the old, who, after retirement, have little means of sustaining their income. There was a time when they could have relied on the iron rice bowl to provide them with a pension. But that no longer applies. Deng's new era reforms, with their emphasis upon incentives, ended these guarantees. State pensions are paid from taxes and in China the taxation system is a baffling mess. There is no clear-cut pattern of income or corporation tax; regions vary in the way and level at which they are taxed. The lack of uniformity is an encouragement to corruption. Pensions seem to be in crisis in all modern countries, where ageing populations are putting increasing strains on the working population who alone can provide the funds to pay the pensions. The problem is particularly acute in China where by the middle of this century over a third of the Chinese people will be over retirement age. It is highly unlikely that China will ever be able to develop a workable national pension scheme. Since it is the aged who are the poorest, this means that poverty is ineradicable in many parts of China.

11

pollution in China

This chapter will cover:
- the Three Gorges Dam Project
- the extent of the pollution problem
- the damage to health standards
- attempts to deal with the problem
- the unlikelihood of finding a solution.

The Three Gorges Dam Project

The 77-year-old Gong Wanqing looked at the house where generations of his family had lived for over 400 years. It was 30 January 2006. The following day he would have to leave all this. The waters of the Yangzi would soon rise and drown the land on which he stood. He turned to look up the hill to where his new home stood. 'Our new house is ready, but we just don't want to go,' he said as the tears poured down his cheeks.

Gong Wanqing's story represents the fate of millions of Chinese who have become victims of the Three Gorges Dam Project. Nothing illustrates the power of the Communist government in China more vividly than this enterprise. Begun in 1994 and largely completed by June 2006, the £15 billion project is expected by 2008 to be supplying some 30 million people in 28 cities with a total of 85 billion kilowatts of hydro-electric energy. Nor is it simply a matter of energy provision. The dam's massive locks lift ships 185 metres vertically thus allowing vessels of up to 10,000 tons to travel a further 400 miles up the Yangzi as far as Chongqing. This connects the interior of China with ports throughout the world, so enabling China's coal, steel, cars, IT equipment, and the myriad trinkets, toys and gadgets that it produces to flood the markets of the world.

The project was the brain-child of Li Peng, who, as prime minister and hard-liner in the Maoist mould, first proposed it in 1992. It is presented as a stupendous success by the Chinese government, and there is no denying that in its conception and construction it is a breathtaking example of applied national ambition. The design and engineering skills involved in it have excited international admiration. But it has come at an enormous cost. From the beginning it has had its critics, even within the party and government. In a very rare example of a publicly admitted dispute within the Communist Party, a number of the delegates to the National people's Conference in 1992 declined to support the plan for the Three Gorges Project. The concern of those who either opposed or abstained in the vote was that the scale of the project would cause vast social and economic disruption in the areas affected by the building of the dams and the raising of the level of the Yangzi River.

Their fears proved well founded. Disregarding objections from the communities affected, the government went through with plans for the uprooting and resettlement of huge numbers of people. Towns and villages were given notice to quit their homes by a certain date. The bulldozers then moved in and razed every building. Here and there some residents refused to move, claiming they did not wish to live in the new tower blocks built elsewhere for them; they would rather stay and live in the rubble of their old homes. But such resistance proved no more than a pathetic gesture; the rising flood waters forced them up the hillsides.

The latest organized protest came in March 2006, two months before the completion of the dams. Hundreds of farmers, embittered by the loss of their lands and the false promises of the government about the quality of their new accommodation, gathered in Wushan, a port town on the Yangzi. One of their spokesmen declared, 'We were cheated. We tried to build new businesses after we were forced off the land. But I have had to move ten times in three years. The compensation isn't enough to get an adequate home and nobody will listen.' But the authorities were ready for the protesting farmers. Baton-wielding policemen violently attacked and scattered them. During the following week 'political work teams' moved into Wushan to flush out any remaining protesters and sympathizers.

Eventually, the authorities admitted that 1.25 million people had been displaced and relocated, a number that some neutral observers said should be more than doubled in order to give the true picture. What the authorities would not admit was the corruption by the government officials involved in handling the relocation. Every region affected by the project had stories to tell of bungs and kick-backs, bribes and blackmail, all carried out against a background of state intimidation.

In addition to the social turmoil, personal suffering and corruption there has been a heavy environmental price to pay. Up to 8,000 archaeological sites have been submerged; to this cultural catastrophe has to be added an ecological disaster. The polluted remains of some 1,500 factories have also disappeared under the waters. This has had a disastrous effect on the fish and bird life of the region.

One cannot imagine any other major nation permitting, let alone completing such a scheme. Leaving aside the disruption of millions of lives, the environmental issue alone would have made the project unacceptable. But such is the power of the central government that it has pushed through its scheme with little initial resistance. It has exploited a 4,000-year-old Chinese tradition that requires the people to obey the dictates of central

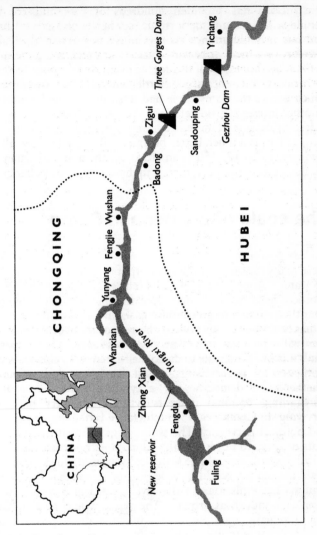

figure 8 the Three Gorges Dam

authority. Even when those affected woke up to what was going on their belated protests were suppressed or ignored.

But if there are losers, there are also winners. This is a fact that relates to all China's modern developments. The massive construction has provided hundreds of thousands of local people with jobs and opportunities where none existed before and has brought money to previously poverty-stricken areas. Nor has provision of better housing been simply a government myth. The distress of those forced from their homes has to be set against the successful resettlement of many communities which before the dams came had lived in wretched conditions. Another interesting side effect is the boost given to the world's oldest profession. One entrepreneur gloated: 'I used to be a farmer. This is a much better business – I've got 15 girls, all nice students, 17 to 18. 250 yuan (£15) for them and 50 yuan (£3) for me, at least five customers a night – it's very busy here now.'

The scale of pollution in China

China has 30,000 working coal mines. It is building one new nuclear power station every year and by 2010 will have 30 of these in operation. Its pollution output is greater than that of the USA and Europe put together. Its refusal to sign the 1997 Kyoto Protocol has effectively destroyed the international attempt to limit the emission of greenhouse gases. If China will not sign up it makes little difference what the rest of the world does. Why then will China not sign? The answer is simple. China does not think it is in its interests to do so. Self-interest, of course, is what motivates all governments in all countries. A government, whether in a democracy or a tyranny, that is seen to be disregarding national interests will have a very hard time surviving. In China's case, its reluctance is not simple economic and political perversity. The wellsprings of its attitude lie deep in its history. To put it bluntly; China does not trust the outside world. Indeed, it would be historically accurate to say that it has never trusted the world outside. China argues that if it were to limit its gas emissions to the level agreed at Kyoto it would cripple its industrial growth. The result would be that China would remain poor for ever while the developed countries would continue to live comfortably.

Since the early 1990s, some 15 million acres of farmland have been turned into urban sprawl as industrial sites proliferate. Occasionally the central and local authorities talk earnestly of the need to conserve and preserve. But their heart is not in it. Nothing has been allowed to stand in the way of economic growth. The world was shocked in 1997 at the time of the Kyoto international agreement on controlling carbon emissions by two revelations: one was the sheer scale of environmental pollution in China; the second was the realization that China was not prepared to do anything about it. Interestingly the other great nation that declined to sign up to the Kyoto Protocol was the United States. Neither China nor the USA was prepared to have its economic growth restricted and controlled by an agreement drawn up by other nations whose goodwill and true intentions were not to be trusted. China let it be known that it would not take lectures from the West on preserving the environment. The Chinese view is that it is hypocritical of the Western nations, who have made themselves wealthy by exploiting the world's resources with nary a thought as to environmental damage, should now seek to pressure China into adopting policies that would slow its growth. To add weight to this assertion, the Chinese pointed out that the resources and fuel used in flying the delegates to Kyoto and in the junketing that accompanied the conference would have maintained a Chinese town for over a year.

Yet there were signs by 2006 that the PRC was becoming more sensitive about the environmental issues attached to such phenomenal growth. In the planning of new towns, greater thought was being given to the harmful effects that uncontrolled expansion can bring. In a major development, planned to take pressure off Shanghai, building began on a series of suburbs which will become towns in themselves. One of these is an area called Dongtan. Designed by the British company, Arup, it will arise from paddy fields, to become an 'eco-city'. A selection of housing is planned, which will range from luxury dwellings for the affluent to low-cost apartments for the workers. The buildings will be constructed from sustainable materials and open spaces, waterways and recreational areas will form an integral part of the development. Dongtan will grow in controlled stages to become a city of nearly one million by the middle of the century. Arup's Chinese spokesman declared, 'We want to demonstrate in what way this can happen without destabilizing the world in terms of emissions, pollution and resources.' It remains doubtful whether projects such as Dongtan can succeed and, if they can, whether they will simply be exceptions to the frantic rush that has so far characterized Chinese industrial and urban growth, interesting as experiments, certainly, but not to be widely adopted. It is difficult to believe that the PRC would seriously consider limiting its growth just to conform to environmental standards arbitrarily laid down by international bodies that it does not believe have China's needs and interests at heart.

Destruction in the cities

The minister of culture, Sun Jiazheng, admitted in 2006 that his country's record on heritage preservation was not a happy one. He acknowledged, for example, that Beijing, the capital, had not been sufficiently protected from the developers' bulldozer. He did not refer to, although he may have had in mind, the disappearance of the *hutong*. These were grey stone alleyways that linked the tiny one-level houses in which most ordinary Beijingers lived. The *hutong* existed in their many thousands and gave a distinctive character to the city. Many were demolished in the 1950s to clear the way for the construction of Tiananmen Square. Even more have gone since. Almost 6,000 *hutong* were destroyed in the decade between 1996 and 2005. In their place stand high-rise apartment blocks where the upwardly mobile who are building the new China now live.

Until recently one of the *hutong* areas seemingly safe from the threat of demolition was Qianmen located at the southern end of Tiananmen Square. The government had promised that Qianmen was one of 25 areas that, because of their historical value, would be protected. But the government has reneged on its promise. Its excuse is that the need to have Beijing ready for the 2008 Olympics has forced a change of plan. This does not convince the Qianmen locals, who see it all as part of the corruption that pervades construction and development in Beijing. One resident said that he and his family had been offered the equivalent of £27,000 to move, but this was a drop in the ocean compared to the millions that the housing officials would make from the sale of the site. Some locals have resolved to resist by refusing to move. But even the most determined of them know that this can be only a gesture. They know from the experience of all the other *hutong* dwellers that their homes will be knocked down around them, and that they will be forced to accept the government's non-negotiable offer of compensation and resettlement in an area over which they have no choice.

Even though Sun Jiazheng publicly regretted such state vandalism, it is difficult to view his words as other than a public relations exercise put on to convince the Chinese and impress foreigners that China is taking conservation seriously. It is not. And the reason is simple. The government derives so much money from selling land leases to developers that it is never going to take genuine steps to restrict their activities. A vivid example of this is the fate that befell the village of Yangee near Beijing. Judging it to be a prime area for residential development that would attract the wealthier Beijing yuppies, a property tycoon bribed the region's local government to lease him the land on which the village stood. The inhabitants were not consulted; they were denied adequate compensation and were simply ordered to leave. When they refused, they were driven out by armed police who were quite prepared to break heads with batons. The developer then proceeded to build 1,000 luxury housing units, whose individual asking price in 2006 was equivalent to £600,000.

The authorities also used violence in Guangdong, one of the SEZs. To the government's dismay Guangdong, a flagship of the new China, has experienced disturbing social unrest and disorder. In 2005 over 20 local people were shot dead during the suppression of a demonstration against the forcible seizure of their lands. The basic grievance is that venal state officials make corrupt deals with the developers and totally disregard claims for compensation from the dispossessed. Villagers described with fury how after working away from home for months at a time in order to provide for their wives and children, they would return to find that their houses had been knocked down and their families left without shelter.

Losing the conservation battle

There are committed conservationists within China who try to spread the message of the need to recognize and limit the great environmental damage that China's headlong dash for growth is inflicting on itself and the world. They quote frightening statistics: China has five of the world's ten most polluted cities; 120 million Chinese live in cities breathing toxic air that is shortening their lives; two-thirds of China's rivers are so polluted by chemical waste that fish cannot live in them; thousands of acres of fruitful land are being turned into desert every month; hundreds of species of plant and animal life disappear every year. Their often courageous work has its successes. National government and local authorities regularly make reference to the need for conservation and claim that all new projects will have to meet set environmental standards. A group led by Professor Lei of Beijing University monitored the development of the Three Gorges Dam Project from its beginning and used its knowledge and data to influence the government to make certain changes that reduced some of the project's more environmentally destructive features.

The government makes much in official statements about its resolve to tackle the problem. It has established a series of regulations and requirements that on paper look very impressive. But inspection is haphazard and unsystematic. Factories often receive inside information warning them that an inspection is coming so that they can do a quick clean-up job. Occasionally companies are called to account for failure to meet set standards, but even when penalties are imposed they seem mere tokens. There is an air of unreality about it all. The government does not want to kill the golden goose that provides so much revenue and gives China its industrial growth. There is no government anti-pollution programme that is comparable with the scale of the problem. It is as if Mao's Great Leap Forward had been restarted with the same disregard for the harmful consequences.

People regarded as heroes by Chinese and international conservationists are usually seen by locals as interfering troublemakers intent on damaging the prospects of prosperity coming to their region. The big companies not only please the central government by contributing large tax revenues, they bring a great deal of wealth into the community. Few locals are going to sniff at that just to satisfy some fanatical green lobbyists. The battle between developers and conservationists may be regarded as a form of civil war in which all the big guns are on the side of the developers.

China's conservationists are heroic figures but they are isolated and they are fighting a battle against such odds that they have no realistic chance of overturning the government. The truth is that China's industrial growth is such a colossal venture with so many vested interests tied up in its maintenance and success that protesters, even when they produce measured, scientifically verified evidence of the damage being caused, seldom win the big battles. Even when the government appears to listen to green pressure groups and makes concessions in the form of new restrictions on development, these are subsequently ignored. Bringing polluters to account is not easy. Experience suggests that they have little to fear. The transgressors are often hand in glove with government officials, and the courts are not truly independent. The Communist Party's big worry is not the spread of pollution. Rather, it is that if its great programme of economic growth is slowed it will have failed in the task it set itself of modernizing China. If that should happen it would be left with no justification for its rule over the Chinese people.

The cancer villages

The figures which the government has been unable to suppress make disturbing reading. A study conducted between 1995 and 2005 by a group of Hong Kong universities calculated that 1,600 of the city's inhabitants died every year from sicknesses brought on or worsened by air pollution. This statistic is unsurprising to those who have witnessed the pall of smog that periodically envelops Hong Kong when the prevailing winds bring the accumulated pollution of the coal-fired plants and factories of southern China to mix with the exhaust fumes of the city's grid-locked traffic. Elsewhere figures have revealed that many rivers and their tributaries are polluted by industrial waste. In addition nine out of ten cities are dependent on groundwater which is polluted. The result is that 300 million Chinese have to drink poisoned water. Of these nearly 200 million have become sick. One of the most tragic aspects of this is that each year this century 30,000 children have died from diarrhoea. A report in May 2006 estimated that within five years 70 per cent of the Yangzi, China's greatest river, will be toxic.

When people fall seriously ill it is extremely difficult for them or their families to gain compensation. Companies and officials invariably unite in denying that pollution was the specific cause of any of the diseases contracted. In the rare instances where the matter gets to court, the claimants have to provide expert medical evidence to establish their case. This is either simply not obtainable or so expensive as to be beyond their means. Moreover, legal hearings tend to drag on over years. In today's China 'the law's delay' is as much a scandal as it was in Hamlet's Denmark.

The worst affected areas have become known as 'cancer villages'. They are a product of the headlong rush for growth in China since the 1980s. Too little care went into the planning of the spreading towns and factories. No thought was given to balancing industrial expansion with the needs of those living in the areas under development. One of the worst cases recorded is the village of Xiditou near the port of Tianjin, 100 miles south of Beijing. A quarter of Xiditou's 1,000 residents have developed cancer over the last ten years. In cold figures, this is 30 times greater than the national average for contracting the disease. The village is a stinking mess. Paint factories empty their effluent into the streams and rivers on which they have been sited. The flow of water has slowed as banks of black sludge grow daily. On certain days, a miasma visibly fills the air and shrouds the village in a dark pall. One resident said despairingly: 'We used to be famous for our rice. Now the water is so bad that we cannot sell our local vegetables. We are told they do not pass national safety standards.'

The physical pollution was matched by political corruption. Initially the bewildered villagers had not understood what was happening to them. When they began to suspect their illnesses were caused by the toxic waste they were pressured by the authorities to say nothing. Not wishing to damage the lucrative arrangements they had made with the private developers and factory owners, local officials would not take up the villagers' claim for compensation. Nor was help forthcoming when the villagers tried to use the local courts to recover the money they had paid out for medical treatment. Despite gaining evidence from a Beijing University research team that the tap water contained strong traces of benzene that put it 50 per cent above national safety levels, the claimants were told their cases were not worth proceeding with.

Far from being an exceptional case, Xiditou has proved all too typical of rural experience. Pollution and environmental damage are spreading not diminishing in China. Occasionally the regional authorities have responded by closing plants that have clearly damaged a locality. But these apparently firm measures are window dressing, a pretence. They are haphazard and unco-ordinated and in no sense represent a national anti-pollution plan. The plain truth is there are too many powerful interests involved for a proper clean-up campaign to be maintained successfully. Government, both local and national, land grabbers and developers and industrial companies have too much to gain from the present situation. In addition, workers for whom industrial growth means a job with regular wages are reluctant to support environmental schemes that threaten their livelihood by closing factories down. All this is a bleak prospect for China.

The PRC's reluctance to mount a genuine attack on pollution

Such is the rate of the spread of China's dust bowl that, within decades, the Gobi desert will have reached Beijing. Already in winter there are days in the capital when clouds of desert dust blown on the wind block out the sun and the people hide their faces in smog masks. Across the land there are many government-backed schemes for tree planting and land reclamation but these have an air of desperation about them. Pessimists say it is all too little, too late.

Nor is it merely Beijing and China that are threatened. Pollution is China's largest export. Tibet's rivers poisoned by industrial waste flow into India and Bangladesh. Sulphur deposits from China's coal mines drop as far west as the Black Sea. An extraordinary statistic is that one-third of the people of the world use water from China. Acid rain from China's factories falls on Korea, Japan and South East Asia. Toxic dust from China's factories has been known to reach Canada.

Why does China not take steps to stop this? The reason is frighteningly simple. If China were to take conservation and anti-pollution seriously every year it would have to spend on its clean-up programme the equivalent of what it derives from its annual growth rate of around 8 per cent. The equation is in exact balance. To put it another way; to go green China would have to give up being a modern industrial power. Understandably, it is something China simply will not contemplate. Bitter though this is for conservationists worldwide to accept, the reality is that China's refusal to cut its pollution output means that plans made elsewhere to clean up the planet are doomed to be of only minimal effect. China in the end will not be told what to do. Its sense of historical grievance applies strongly here. It believes that it was previously the victim of imperialist exploitation by western nations who cared little then for China's well-being. Why, it asks, should China now listen to the pleas of its former exploiters who, having made themselves rich without a thought as to the environmental consequences of what they were doing, have suddenly developed qualms? China will not limit its growth merely so that the West can unburden itself of its bad conscience. It is an argument that appeals powerfully to Chinese nationalism.

12

religion in China

This chapter will cover:
- China's religious traditions
- the PRC's suppression of religion
- religious revival in China
- the overlap of religion and politics
- the CCP's crisis of identity.

Religion in Communist China

Few things give as clear an insight into the character of a nation as its attitude towards religion. Mao Zedong once told the Dalai Lama that religion was a poisonous plant and that Christian missionaries in China were hated in the same way as the Nazis came to be universally loathed. Chinese Communism, as with all forms of Marxism, regards religion as dangerous nonsense; nonsense because it is based on unscientific superstitious notions, deliberately spread by the powerful classes to keep the workers in their place; dangerous because it encourages doubts about the perfect secular society that Communism is dedicated to creating. Ironically, what Communism itself most closely resembles is a secular religion. It claims to have discovered the basic truths about the human condition, and, because it has made this discovery, to have the right to exercise absolute authority. Those who dare challenge this authority are guilty of a form of political heresy and are not to be tolerated. It was such thinking that has made the PRC so sensitive on religious issues. What Chinese Communism recognized in religion was its mirror image.

That is why, since 1949, when the authorities have allowed the various religious faiths to practise openly it has been only under strict conditions. Organized religion is state controlled. The official line is that a faith is safeguarded provided it does not endanger the security of the state. It is the latter point that enables the PRC to step in and crush any movement that it regards as dangerous. The PRC is currently disturbed by the spread of 'house churches', private dwellings where people of Christian or other faiths gather for meditation and worship. The government finds it very hard to understand why people should want to do such a thing and concludes that it must be a cover for hatching plots and spreading false information about the communist system. Worshippers whose homes have been invaded and ransacked by the police are likely to be dumped in labour camps. State television broadcasts scenes of police raids on 'house churches', unashamedly claiming that this is further proof of how the government actively and resolutely hunts down the enemies of the people.

Problems for the authorities

However, religion is so deep-rooted in Chinese tradition that it has never been possible for China's Communist rulers to undermine it totally. The three major religions of Chinese tradition are Taoism, Confucianism and Buddhism and they continue to be highly influential in China. Part of their strength is that they have not competed with each other. Often, indeed, they became merged in practice and people claimed happily that they were both Confucians and Buddhists. The faiths have much in common. Buddhism, with its stress on the attaining of inner enlightenment, sits easily with the Taoist pursuit of the way and the Confucian search for virtue through harmony. What they share is the capacity to make a cruel world more bearable. For millennia they have shaped Chinese thinking. Set against them Marxism seems a philosophical upstart.

Many Chinese have inherited a very inclusive attitude to religion. Their approach to it is often very practical. Some are prepared to try various religions to see which one suits them best, as if it were a piece of clothing. As a taxi-driver in Fuzhou in Futian province cheerfully said, 'Yes, I used to be a Christian but it didn't work too well, so I switched back to Buddhism.' This is not to be confused with dilettantism. Rather it is a willingness to search for a pattern of thought that suits the individual's spiritual or emotional needs.

Under Mao, foreign faiths, most notably Christianity and Islam, were lumped together with home grown philosophies like Buddhism and Confucianism to be condemned and prohibited as superstitions that had no place in revolutionary China. During the Cultural Revolution, Confucianism was denounced as representing all that was worst in China's past. However, it is always difficult to stamp out a religion. Repressive regimes are able to suppress the outward expressions of belief, but it is much harder to crush the belief itself. All China's major faiths survived Mao's persecution. The post-Mao Communist Party has had to be much more circumspect in its approach to the religious issue. This is because a religious revival has occurred; there are reckoned to be 60 million Christians and as many Muslims in China. Together with some 200 million Buddhists, these form a substantial minority.

When religious activities are held to threaten national security or stability, suppression is still the ultimate government weapon, but the authorities have also tried to prevent problems arising in the first place. This has been done by encouraging the development of what are called the 'patriotic churches'. These are, in effect, state churches whose members are allowed to worship publicly provided that they accept their doctrines and clergy being vetted by the authorities. The government tries to play upon believers' sense of patriotism and nationalism and get them to regard their churches as an expression of their love of China. This is the notion behind the 'three self churches': self-governing, self-propagating and self supporting. Here the government's aim is to persuade the worshippers to reject outside influences. Why, they ask, should good Chinese be influenced by rules laid down by foreign religious leaders who are the heirs to the Western imperialists of old who once held China in subjection?

The appeal of Christianity to modern Chinese

A tactic of the government that runs in tandem with its repressive measures is to make light of religion as if it were something whimsical and fanciful, having little to do with China's real needs. It suggests that religion for those in their teens and twenties has become something of a fashion accessory, and it is certainly true that in the early 2000s there were young Chinese who considered it 'cool' to be religious, in rather the same way that in the Beatles' era in the West in the 1960s eastern mystic religions became very fashionable with America's and Europe's young.

The authorities have also attempted to ridicule Christianity by saying that it is a religion for backward rural women. They point out that 75 per cent of Chinese Christians are female, and that 65 per cent of Christians live in the countryside. Yet there is a deeper aspect to it. The government's figures were correct for the year 2000 but the proportions are changing. Many more males are converting to Christianity. Nor is it simply a matter of numbers. There are groups of intellectuals referred to as 'Cultural Christians' who are not baptised and do not formally worship but who have a great philosophical interest in religion. These mainly belong to the 30–50 age group, and are some of the brightest of China's urban population. They are people who were taught at school and university that atheism was the only true outlook for committed Communists. But, finding little in Marxism that could explain or help them to come to terms with the rapid change that China has undergone over the last 30 years, they have tended to swing away from that form of political absolutism to look for satisfaction in a faith that can offer spiritual and intellectual satisfaction in the face of growing state-sponsored materialism. Those who were most indoctrinated in

Marxism are those who now appear to find Christianity most appealing. They continue to look for answers to the big questions in life that Chinese Communism seems unable to furnish. There are some 40 universities in China that now offer courses on Western religion and theology, a remarkable figure when one considers that 40 years ago religion itself was outlawed during the Cultural Revolution. It supports the observation that there is a feeling among educated Chinese that, since Marxism has fallen short of its promise, it is time to turn back to those Western values that Marxism attacked. The religious problem in China is a striking illustration of that love–hate relationship that China has had with the West ever since the days of European domination in the nineteenth century.

The Buddhist revival

China's own traditional faiths are also flourishing. In April 2006 in Hangzhou, representatives of the Buddhist communities throughout China came together with members of the faith from 30 other countries in a world forum. The theme was harmony and the harmonious society, which is why the authorities were prepared to allow the gathering to take place in China. The significance of the forum went beyond religion. It was a statement by China's Buddhists that they wished to play their part in the development of China as a nation. Discussions on economics, the environment and human rights formed part of the programme. While the forum was careful not to criticize the government openly, many of the things said were critical by implication, such as the suggestion that the world's people, including the Chinese, were looking for a sense of purpose in their lives. This was why China's official newspapers either ignored the forum or reported it in a dismissive way.

Beijing's clash with the Vatican

The trouble that China's religious revival can cause for the government, in foreign as well as domestic affairs, is evident in the clash between Beijing and the Roman Catholic Church. The Vatican claims that the Church in China is effectively under the control of the Chinese government that demands the final say in the appointment of bishops. As a protest against this interference, the Vatican formally recognized Taiwan as the true

China. By 2006, seven mainland Chinese bishops who would not co-operate with the authorities had either disappeared or were under house arrest. This is why the Papacy refuses to recognize any new bishops who have not been first been approved by the Vatican.

The reasons for Rome–Beijing tensions are not hard to understand. Under Mao, Catholics were persecuted; their churches were closed and their priests and nuns imprisoned. If any Catholics still wished to practise their faith openly and legally they had to join the 'Patriotic Association', a body created and run by the Communists that recognized Mao and the CCP as the only proper authority, not the Papacy. As one Catholic put it: 'I won't go to the state-controlled church but I will attend any church that has the Pope as its leader. If that means praying at home, I don't see anything wrong with that. We are not concerned with superficialities. During the Cultural Revolution we all prayed at home even though the state didn't allow religion. Religion caters to your soul.'

There were hopes on both sides in the post-Mao years that relations would improve. But a basic problem remained for the PRC. To give in to the demand for religious freedom would encourage China's Catholics to switch their loyalties from the Communist Party to a foreign dominated religion. This would give hope to the other main religions in China – Islam and Buddhism – that they, too, could develop independently of the State. Pluralism, the acceptance of religious and cultural diversity, which is a highly attractive concept in progressive societies, frightens the Chinese leaders.

Superstition

There is also a worrying development for the authorities in that many rural Chinese, disorientated by the recent rapid changes in China that have destroyed their old ways, are turning to superstition to fill the emptiness. Superstition has always had a prominent place in Chinese life. Taoist temples do not have their own shrines to be venerated. They are receptacles for what worshippers bring. Many are now filled with trinkets, pictures and statues that many ordinary people deposit there to bring them good luck and good health. All this may seem harmlessly irrational, but observers suggest that it illustrates how people, having lost a moral compass, are putting increasing faith in a providence that they feel may not be entirely blind. It is a reaction, perhaps an unwitting one in many cases, against the materialism that threatens to overtake China and that the Communist system encourages.

As a one-party state with a single dominant ideology, the PRC has no time for strongly held beliefs, whether religious or political, that undermine the cohesion of Communist China. But the PRC is faced with the problem that confronts all systems based on essentially secular values. It has proved easier for the Communist government to condemn religion as mere superstition than it is to offer an alternative that people find as emotionally and culturally satisfying.

The campaign against the Falun Gong

The trouble for the state in persecuting religion is that it often has the reverse effect of the one intended. It can encourage rather than deter. Some believers take great comfort from the parallel between their situation in China and that of the early Christian Church which in spite of, perhaps because of, its persecution by the Roman Empire grew stronger not weaker. The blood of the martyrs nourishes the seeds of faith.

Yet the response of the Communist government to ideas it does not understand is still to prohibit them and persecute those who hold them. A case in point is the attempted suppression of the Falun Gong. This movement, which began in 1992, is very much part of the Taoist–Buddhist tradition; it holds that mind and body are one and are best developed by spiritual and physical exercises that give the practitioner emotional peace, expressed in the watchwords 'Truthfulness, Compassion and Forbearance'. Initially tolerant of the Falun Gong, the authorities soon began using a mixture of strong-arm tactics and propaganda to discredit and break up what was officially described as an 'evil cult'. In April 2006 a member of the Falun Gong caused a scene when she gate-crashed a White House reception in honour of China's visiting official representative, Hua Jiabo. Before security staff could hustle her away she had shouted at Hua that he was murdering Falun Gong members in China, and tearfully appealed to President Bush to denounce these crimes.

Problems in the Muslim provinces

Since its formation in 1949 the PRC has consistently denied the right of any of its regions to break away, claiming that its integrity and strength as a nation depends on maintaining unity and central control. This attitude has brought its dangers. The growing willingness of the Islamic world to flex its muscles in the twenty-first century means problems for China, which contains a significant number of Muslims among its population. These are particularly numerous among the Uighur people in Xinjiang, a province of north-west China. Xinjiang, which is as large as western Europe, is bordered on its western side by eight separate countries. Worryingly for China, most of these countries, which include Pakistan, Tajikistan and Kazakhstan, are strongly Muslim. Beijing's realistic fear is that religion is combining with politics to create a dangerous movement for Xinjiang independence. There have already been serious disturbances in the region, which Beijing blames on troublemakers and infiltrators from Tajikistan. As it did in Tibet, the PRC originally tried to weaken the independence movement in Xinjiang by settling millions of Chinese in the region.

The policy has not been entirely successful. In a situation reminiscent of the troubles in the Middle East, China has to maintain a strong military presence and tight border controls in an ongoing attempt to prevent terrorist incursions. The PRC claims that the 200 or so major terrorist acts that have occurred, which include indiscriminate bombing and planned assassinations, are the work of a tiny, unrepresentative minority of the many ethnic groups that make up the region's population. The government's official line is that its purpose in Xinjiang, as in the other provinces of China, is to advance the interests of all the region's peoples, the great majority of whom are totally opposed to independence.

The social value of religion

The Communist government is sharply aware of the lack of a powerful bonding force now among the Chinese people. By allowing China to embrace capitalist methods as the only means by which the nation could be modernized, the Communists took a risk whose consequences are now hard, perhaps impossible, to avoid. If national economic growth and individual profit making is now legitimate, indeed, not merely legitimate but actively promoted by the government as life's chief purpose, then what is left of revolutionary idealism? How are the people to be inspired? The rush to get rich quick, which has created a materialist, yuppie mind-set, has not been good for the human spirit. Churches find that people are turning to them, not for theology in which the Chinese have never been especially interested, but for spiritual sustenance. The language in which worshippers refer to each as other as brothers and sisters appeals to the Chinese sense of kinship that is being lost in China's vast, anonymous modern cities.

The communist authorities have a split mind over the religious revival that has occurred in China. In one obvious sense it is a threat to the secular values that the Communist Party still formally proclaims. But the party also realizes that its attacks on religion might go too far. Materialism and consumerism have become the modern gods and something is needed to fight them. Religion has qualities that the government are desperate to see restored to China. The speed of change in the new era has produced a moral vacuum. Appalled by the venality they see around them, there are Chinese, some at the top level, who say that it is people with religious faith who are the only ones who obey the laws and behave decently. They do not embezzle, cheat or open brothels in their back rooms.

There has also been something of an upswing in Mao's reputation. This is not because of his politics; the authorities cite his principles and sayings as the basis on which people, particularly the disruptive young, should conduct themselves. Confucianism, too, is back in fashion; the government urge the people to respect the Chinese traditions of restrained behaviour and social decorum. The appeal now is for the restoration of a harmonious society. In an Alice-in-Wonderland move, the Chinese government has earmarked £120 million to be spent on rebuilding Beijing's ancient temples and shrines that it has spent generations knocking down.

The CCP's dilemma

The trouble for Chinese Communism as an atheistic system is that it has little with which it can match the spiritual appeal of the religion to which the people are turning. But it is not simply a question of trying to convince the people of the continuing worth of the Communist system. There are distinct signs of a crisis of political faith within the Communist Party itself. A parallel can be drawn between the Communist Party in China now and the Communist Party in the Soviet Union before its fall in the early 1990s. Those in authority still pay lip service to Communism as a social theory, but nobody really believes in it any more. It survives as a governmental mechanism that guarantees that the party stays in power and that its members continue to enjoy the privileges it confers. But Communism has lost it power to inspire.

Previously, whatever excesses and errors may have been committed by the Communist governments, believers in Chinese Communism as a movement could always take comfort from the thought that the intentions and motives were right. Equality and fair shares for the people were the aim and purpose of the party. But with the reforms of the Deng era came a desire for material gains. Economic growth based on capitalist economic methods swamped the inspiring social objectives. The sense of comradeship and common purpose that was such a characteristic of revolutionary China is dying. This raises the question of how long it will be before the internal contradictions of Chinese Communism bring it to crisis point. It seems unlikely to be able to maintain itself permanently in power.

13

women in modern China

This chapter will cover:
- traditional Chinese attitudes towards women
- continuing female exploitation
- threats to family life from modernization
- China's population policy
- signs of progress.

The place of women in imperial China

If the status and treatment of women are taken as measures of social progress, then it has to be said that China has yet to become fully modern. Imperial China was a society that discriminated against women. In Confucian thought, social harmony depended on maintaining the *san gang*, the three relationships that bound society together: the loyalty of ministers and officials to the emperor, the respect of children for their parents, and the obedience of wives to their husbands. Occasionally women took a prominent place in affairs, as with Cixi, the Empress Dowager who in effect ruled for most of the last 20 years of the Qing dynasty. But for the most part women played a subordinate role.

Mao Zedong's early life offers some fascinating examples of how restricted women's lives were in old China. His own mother did not have a name but a number; she was called Wen Qimei, which translates simply as 'seventh daughter'. At the age of 14, Mao was informed by his father that a betrothal had been arranged for him; Mao was to marry a 20-year-old woman from a nearby village. Arranged marriages were customary in imperial China. Love and compatibility did not come into it. The arrangement was economic. The boy's family paid money to the girl's family, the amount being calculated on how many children she was likely to produce. The benefit for the groom's family was that they gained, in effect, an unpaid domestic servant since the usual practice was for the bride to become a skivvy under her mother-in-law's orders. Mao rejected all this; he declined to co-operate in the matchmaking even when his father told him the bride-price had already been paid.

Later official Chinese Communist Party accounts of this incident usually depicted it as an example of Mao's early struggle against an iniquitous marriage system in which women were bought and sold. Mao's real motives were probably not wholly idealistic. He may well have regarded the arrangement as his father's way of tying him down and keeping him on the farm. It may also be that at 14 he simply did not like the older woman who had been chosen for him. Mao remained unmoved by his family's pleas that he reconsider, and the match fell through. Mao had successfully defied his father and Chinese social convention.

In 1919 when he was in his twenties Mao became involved in a case that caused a great scandal in Changsha, the capital of his home province. Zhao Wuzhen, the beautiful 23-year-old daughter of the Zhao family, had finally agreed to marry the man her parents had chosen for her. It had been a struggle. Wuzhen at first had been unwilling. She found her intended husband old, ugly and boorish. But he had money; he came from a wealthy merchant family. The arranged marriage would bring her own family added status and income. So Wuzhen had swallowed her pride and her distaste and said yes. On the wedding morning crowds of well-wishers lined the streets and lanes. They clapped and cheered as the sedan chair with the bride inside was carried from her home to the house where the wedding ceremony would take place. As was customary, the curtains of the sedan chair were drawn; it was considered bad luck to see the bride on her journey. The first sight of her in her resplendent gown of red, the bridal colour in China, would be when she stepped out to be greeted by her husband. But when the chair was set down Wuzhen did not step out. She could not. When the curtains were drawn back she was found slumped and gasping and covered in blood. She had slashed her throat with a jagged shard of pottery that she had hidden in her wedding dress. For two hours helpers frantically tried to staunch the bleeding, but Wuzhen was beyond saving. She drowned to death in her own blood.

The suicide divided Changsha between those who believed Wuzhen had betrayed her family and those who felt she had been true to her own honour. Mao did not argue it in these terms. He rushed into print to condemn 'the rottenness of the marriage system and the darkness of the social system' that had forced the young woman into killing herself. He defined arranged marriages as 'indirect rape' and demanded that they be outlawed. Chinese women, he wrote, had always been denied 'status in any area of life' and were 'relegated to the dark corners of society'.

This was powerful stuff and suggested that Mao was wholly committed to female emancipation. It is also certainly true that the Communist Party under him formally declared that women were equal. It made a particular point of abolishing the practice of foot binding that was still to be found in parts of China as late as the 1940s. Yet feminists have pointed out that Mao as a person and the Communists as a party were, in practice, far from honouring the principle of female equality that they espoused. Despite rejecting the society of the past, they were, nonetheless, products of it. Despite its official pronouncements,

Chinese Communism operated as a male-dominated system. Even today, few of the important posts in government and party are filled by women.

Exploitation today

Such emancipation as has come women's way has been by default rather than design. Since so many men in rural China now go to work in the cities they have to leave their wives and mothers to run things. Some two-thirds of China's farms are now managed wholly by women. In the course of things women have taken on responsibilities and made decisions that they would not even have been consulted over in the past. It is this that has weakened the traditional dominance of men in Chinese society.

Yet exploitation remains and in some areas has increased. As many women go to the cities as men. They are the daughters and younger sisters of the mothers and older sisters who stay behind to run the farms. They go the factories where work is plentiful but usually poorly paid; legal protection is minimal. Long hours and regimentation are the norm. A typical experience is that of a group of women employees in an electronics factory in Guangdong province. The women there, most of whom live in on-site dormitories, work 12-hour shifts. One of them confided to a foreign journalist: 'We're not allowed to talk between 6.08 in the morning and 6.08 in the evening. That's why I can barely string a sentence together.' In 2006, the workers' individual earnings at the factory were 210 yuan (£15) for a 60-hour week. This is the equivalent of 25p an hour. It is details like these that explain why Chinese manufacturers are able to maintain the low overheads that allow them to undercut the prices of all their international competitors who pay their own workers a proper living wage. However, to put the figures into perspective, it is worth quoting the words of one of the employees at the factory who was asked why she stayed at the job. 'At home my parents work in the fields from dawn to dusk all year and have only 3,000 yuan to show for it. They wind up with a house full of crops and nothing else. I don't think that beats what I am doing.'

Nevertheless, most migrant workers are homesick and put up with their new life because they have little choice. It is this that renders their visits home especially meaningful. In their personal and family relationships the Chinese are not generally a tactile people. Hugging and kissing and open shows of affection are not commonly indulged in publicly, certainly not in rural regions. Instead, family members tend to express their feelings for each other by giving presents. That is why it is so important for migrant workers to take gifts home on their holiday breaks. At such times the Chinese trains that run from the major cities to the stations in the countryside are a remarkable sight. Crammed with people all bearing boxes, packages and bags, which they zealously guard to protect them from damage, the carriages and corridors are a constant scrimmage, good-natured for the most until the cramped conditions and long jolting journeys cause tempers to fray.

Sadly, however, visits home are few, perhaps no more than two a year, and these are often heart-breaking affairs, particularly for the working mothers who count the precious days before they have to leave their young children at home again. In most cases it is the grandparents who bring up the children. Normal family life is becoming increasingly difficult to preserve in modern China. It is as if the middle generation is missing. This is poignantly illustrated in Dazang village in southern China. Dazang is made up of two rows of white-washed single storey houses, each with an odd-looking exposed flight of stairs poking up through the roofs. This is not a local architectural fancy. The stairs were added in the hope that when the children of the household grew up and went to the cities they would return to live and bring up their own families in the second storey that would then be built above their parents' home. But this has not happened. The children have not returned. The stairs that jut upwards are a symbol of China's rural revolution.

Population control

A feature of all modernizing societies has been the encouragement of population control. The notion that increasing population was a threat to the survival of society and nations was accepted by the Chinese Communists. The PRC government introduced a policy based on the assertion that to have more than one child was anti-social, anti-socialist and anti-Chinese. It backed this up with fines and increased taxation on couples who dared to have more. Human rights watchers outside China have condemned this and the still more intrusive measures involving compulsory abortion and sterilization. But the one-child policy has not really worked. Broadly honoured in the urban areas, it has been ignored in many rural regions where families of five or six children remain common. The birth control issue is another mark of the deep divide between rural and industrial China. To limit family size goes against Chinese peasant tradition, which has always regarded large numbers of children as a sign of providence and good fortune as well as a source of extra income. Bureaucratic corruption has also spread to this area. Family planning officials, responsible for imposing fines, have actually encouraged couples to have more children, knowing they will then be able to levy larger sums from them. The fine thus becomes not a disincentive, but a bribe paid to officials to turn a blind eye to the number of children. In Mingxiao, a town in Henan province, officials developed a roaring trade in selling birth permits. As long as the monthly target in fines of 1,500 yuan set for Mingxiao by the central government was met, Beijing was happy to let the local officials make as much as they liked on the side. What the officials did not report to Beijing was that the local birth rate was rocketing not falling.

China's one-child policy

One of the saddest features of Chinese society that lingers is the prejudice against female babies. It is still the wish of most couples to have male children. It is part of the Chinese tradition that saw males as an economic bonus, females as a drain on resources. The government's one-child policy has intensified the problem. Very few want their only child to be a girl. Aware of this, the government did make a concession and permitted parents to have a second child if the first proved to be a girl. But the problem will not go away. Now that scanning techniques can detect the sex of a foetus at an early stage, pregnant women often seek an abortion if the child they are carrying is female. Officially the authorities do not sanction this. Abortion is legal in China but only under certain conditions; termination of foetuses on gender grounds is not one of them. Nevertheless, corruption intrudes here as it does in all areas of officialdom. The all-important birth-planning officer can be bribed. It is this official who keeps records of pregnancies and births and who issues the birth permits for which pregnant women have to apply within five months of conceiving. Her silence and willingness to cook the books can often be bought. Doctors and nurses are also complicit, and private abortion clinics are not difficult to find for those willing to pay.

Disturbing incidents in which female babies, especially if they are disabled, are simply abandoned and left to die grow more numerous. Although there is a register of Chinese couples who are willing to foster rejected infants, it is a matter of chance whether the poor little mites are discovered in time. The bias against girl babies is not simply a tragedy at a personal level. It threatens to be catastrophic for Chinese society overall. Predictions are that by 2020 China will be 40 million women short of what it needs to maintain the balance of society. There simply will not be enough women to become wives and mothers. Pessimists believe that whatever status women may gain from their rarity value will be more than offset by the dangers they will increasingly face as the potential victims of forced marriage, kidnap, trafficking and rape.

Women's vulnerability in urban China

A connected and especially worrying aspect of China's growth is that as the population of the cities explodes, crime is rising. Something of a paradox applies here. Although the authorities are able to exert almost total control in political matters, it is not easy for them to protect ordinary citizens from crime. This is partly because of the anonymity that comes with the growth of urban areas. The number of migrants who come in and their frequent change of address makes it difficult to monitor their movements. This either draws migrants into crime or makes them very vulnerable to it. Lacking knowledge of their surroundings, newcomers are often bewildered and become easy targets for theft and assault. Women are particularly at risk. Cases of abduction and rape increase every year. Girls from the countryside are easy targets. Hundreds, even thousands, of miles from home, and unused to the ways of the city, they accept seemingly genuine offers of help to find accommodation and work, only to discover they have fallen into the often brutal hands of pimps and traffickers. The number of sexual assaults on women and incidences of enforced prostitution grow each year. Matters are not helped by corruption in the police forces. Gangland bosses and racketeers dealing in prostitution and drugs go unmolested as they pay off police officers often at a very high level. Scandals have come to light, revealing that government and party officials are sometimes involved in organized crime.

Yet there is a more positive side to urban life for women. In the cities women have the companionship and mutual support of their female workmates and have access to ways of improving their conditions. Feminist organizations are growing and women are learning to assert themselves and claim the rights that the Communist government insists are theirs. It has been a slow process but is gathering pace. It is clearly evident in many cities that cosmopolitan values have begun replacing traditional Chinese attitudes. Young women in the cities have quickly imbibed foreign ways. Those well-dressed ones who drive, ride or stride confidently to work in Beijing, Shanghai or Guangzhou are barely distinguishable from their counterparts in Paris, London or New York. Book stands at stations and airports are full of women's magazines, all carrying the message that a girl's life is her own to make the best of as she will by refusing to bow before restrictive social convention. The key advice offered to the reader is to think before marrying, since it is marriage that denies women their freedom. Once wed, women fall under the direction of their husband and his family; it is a trap from which it is very difficult to escape. This line is directed particularly at rural women, but it is they who are least likely to receive the message.

Problems in the countryside

Despite the advances in the status of women that the government often proudly pronounces, the lot of many women in China is indeed a grim one. This is true of both town and country but is particularly the case in the rural regions. Married women in the countryside face one of two very unpleasant possibilities. In the first case they become, in effect, the property of their husband and his family. Xie Lihua the editor of the *Rural Women's Magazine*, which is dedicated to changing the attitudes of both women and men in the countryside, describes how precarious life's chances are for women as long as old traditions remain. 'If a woman goes to live with her husband's family and they treat her well, or if she has found someone who loves and respects her, she will be all right. If not things will be very difficult for her. This is because there is a saying among men, "Marrying a woman is like buying a horse – I can ride you and beat you whenever I like."'

In the second case, they are left to fend for themselves if their husband is one of the many men who have left to look for work in the towns. In this case, not only do women manage the farms, but they have all the burdens of family life without adult males to help them. Caring for the young, the old and sick members of the family is a daily responsibility. Huang Yigui, a young woman farmer in Tailian village in central China, described her daily round. 'I get up at four in the morning and work until 7 pm. It's hard. Country life is hard. We are tired. We do it to live, to earn money for us, our children, our parents. I support both old and young. My husband has been working away for over ten years.' Adding to their stress is the knowledge that their husbands working in the cities are likely to drift into extra-marital relationships. There are many distressing cases of women who, having put their heart and soul into trying to keep their scattered family together, long daily for the moment when their husband will return with the money he has saved, only to learn that he is not coming back; he has found another woman and he is spending his savings on his new life with her. Divorce is possible but it is a costly and lengthy process and is still regarded as a disgrace in rural China. Besides, the women's heart and spirit are already broken.

There are figures indicating that four-fifths of rural women suffer from chronic ill-health – a mixture of physical and psychological problems. China has the highest female suicide rate in the world and is the only nation where more women take their own lives than men. Every three and a half minutes, every day, a Chinese woman kills herself; the yearly total is 150,000. Most of these deaths occur in the countryside among women aged between 15 and 25, and the commonest means is the drinking of pesticide. In a piece of black humour, which was at once a comment on the quality of Chinese products and an insight into a particular marriage, a peasant farmer wrote to a chemical company following his wife's failed attempt to kill herself by taking rat poison. 'Thanks to your shoddy pesticide my wife is still alive.'

Mothers in rural China are often a major check on women's freedom. Brought up in the old ways themselves, they tend to be unhappy about their daughters seeking a new way of life. Tradition dies hard; the thought of a young girl going away to work in a distant, strange city is troubling to parents, mothers especially. Whatever its advantages for the daughter in terms of money, experience and education, there is the natural, and justified, fear that she will be harmed or exploited.

Women's status in China's ethnic communities

Up to the present, the restricted role of women in Muslim society has chimed well with China's traditionally male-dominated society. But it may be that, with the infiltration of feminist ideas and China's attempt to give women an equal place, the issue may be an even greater cause of strain between the party and its ethnic minorities. This is markedly evident in the country's western provinces, such as Xinjiang, where the ideas of greater freedom for women have made little headway. Here, in keeping with Muslim tradition, families are very much dominated by the men; women are subject to the orders of husbands, fathers and brothers, and brothers-in-law, and are beaten if they step out of line. There has not been the migration as in other provinces that has taken men away. This has meant that women have not assumed the role of provider and manager. They remain very limited in their experience and aspirations, rarely going outside their village and sometimes not even beyond the front door. Chang Zhen of the All China Women's Federation described their condition as being like a frog in a well: 'All they can see is a tiny bit of sky, so their outlook is very narrow. A woman is treated as a man's possession. It is the duty of a woman to look after him, whether he is working the fields or in the house.' Few of Xijiang's 4 million women escape this crippling tradition. However, if China makes serious official or informal attempts to interfere with this way of life, it is very likely to arouse bitter religious opposition, which may well stimulate the province's separatist movement that Beijing regards with trepidation.

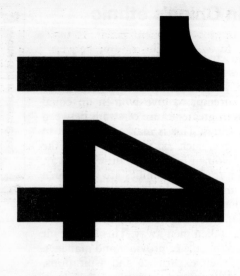

14

China in the twenty-first century – problems and opportunities

This chapter will cover:
- China's industrial revolution
- the problems that have come with economic success
- China's population shift
- problems in education
- the Beijing Olympics, 2008.

China's economic growth

By any measure China's rate of growth is phenomenal. To take one striking set of statistics by way of illustration; between January and December 2005:

- its exports grew in value from $572 billion to $762 billion
- its imports dropped from $770 billion to $660 billion
- its total value of trade rose from $1,065 to $1,420 billion
- its trade surplus tripled from $33 to $102 billion

These figures showed that China was now the world's third largest trading nation, headed only by the USA and Germany. Its economic growth rate has averaged 9 per cent every year since 1981. Further evidence of its remarkable development lies in the fact that China currently devours over a quarter of the world's steel, a third of the world's rice, and nearly half the world's cement. Its consumption of oil is second only to the United States. It is not surprising that everybody wants to trade with China. The opportunities offered by a market of one and a quarter billion people, led by a government committed to commercial expansion in the quickest possible time, make the world's traders and financiers rub their hands in gleeful anticipation.

Between 1978 and 2006, China's exports increased ten-fold. More than 11 per cent of US imports are from China. In a remarkable turn of events that would have been inconceivable in Mao's time, China has become a net creditor of the USA. Against all expectations, the balance of investment is strongly in China's favour; it has, in effect, bought up many American companies. The value of the yuan has climbed against the dollar, a reflection of the huge inflow of Chinese goods into the USA. American manufacturers find it increasingly difficult to compete with their eastern counterparts whose low production costs and wage bills allow them to undercut world prices. It is a remarkable example of how a developing country can cultivate an industrial economy when it does not have to pay decent wages and provide welfare services. Shrewdly, the Chinese have taken measures not to allow the yuan to appreciate too highly. This self-imposed restriction prevents too wide a gap in exchange rates developing; if the yuan became too strong it would out-price Chinese goods in the international market.

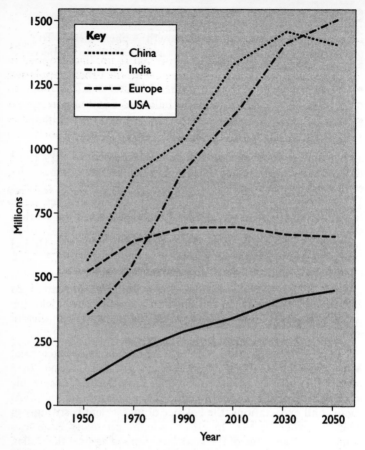

figure 9 world projected population growth by 2050

Population

Figure 9 shows that the figures for China's increase in population are equally remarkable.

To accommodate its teeming people, China in 2006 had some 90 cities of more than 1 million people. The population of Shanghai stood at 17 million; by 2020 it is likely to have risen to 23 million. This vies with Beijing's current population of 18 million, expected to rise to anything between 23 and 30 million by 2020. Dwarfing these is the projected merging of Hong Kong with Guangzhou that will create a 'megalopolis', a continuous urban spread of 60 million people.

As remarkable as the population explosion is the huge shift in the balance between town and country. Half a century ago in Mao's time, over 80 per cent of the Chinese people were peasants living on the land. By 2006 that figure had dropped to 60 per cent. At the current rate of growth, the urban population will overtake the rural somewhere around 2015 and by 2030 town dwellers will number 60 per cent with only 40 per cent left on the land. By 2050 there will be 20 per cent on the land and 80 per cent in the cities, a total inversion of the position 100 years before. It is a social revolution to match anything on the political front. Already the trend has brought great problems as both rural and urban people try to come to terms with their rapidly changing and disorientating world. Thinking of the lines on the graph as two crossing blades, their bewilderment could be called a scissors crisis.

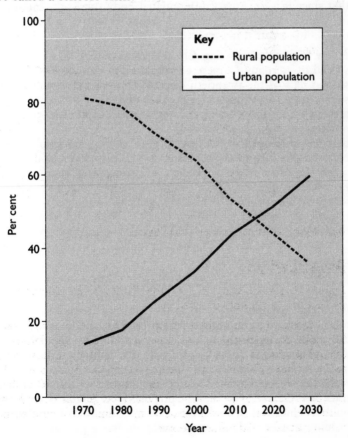

figure 10 China's scissors crisis – the rising urban population, the falling rural population

Trade

In December 2001, after 15 years of negotiation, China joined the World Trade Organization (WTO). This opened up many new markets to China by lifting previous WTO restrictions on Chinese trade. In return, China agreed 'to undertake a series of important commitments to open and liberalize its regime in order to better integrate into the world economy'. The complaint among a number of WTO members is that since it joined the organization China has reaped the benefits but has not always honoured its side of the bargain. The Chinese government disputes this, but the record since 2001 does suggest that it tends to take a one-eyed view, seeing things essentially on its terms. Some in the West have been willing to be understanding of China over this. Critics of the WTO say that since it is an America-dominated body run in the interests of western capitalism, perhaps it is not altogether a bad thing that China treats it irreverently.

A key factor encouraging China's trade growth has been the spread of so many Chinese expatriates throughout Asia in the second half of the twentieth century. Chinese entrepreneurs in such places as Indonesia, Singapore and the Philippines have created a stratum of small and not so small capitalists who, for obvious reasons, are well disposed to the new commercial China that has developed in the last 30 years. China has also shown considerable financial shrewdness. Between 1999 and 2002 when the price of gold fell on the international markets, the British government sold off 13 million ounces, which amounted to nearly half of its of gold reserves. In the same period China bought up nearly 7 million ounces. With the subsequent recovery of gold prices by 2005 Britain found it had lost some £3 billion, equivalent to a penny on the basic tax rate. China in contrast had doubled its money.

It is interesting to note that China also proved far sharper at using the WTO system to its advantage than Britain. In 2006, the British government woke up to the fact that China was selling much more to Britain than it was buying and that Britain's European competitors had also stolen a march. In 2005 Britain's exports to China were worth only £5 billion compared to Germany's £31 billion. In an effort to redress the balance Britain embarked on a major campaign to increase its influence and trade with China. New diplomatic posts were established whose holders' chief task would be to convince China to buy British. Leading figures in the City, including no less a person than the

Mayor of London, were asked to join delegations to carry the message to China of the benefits it could derive by buying into Britain's great experience and expertise in financial matters.

Problems of growth

Although China's economic advance has caught the attention of the world, it should be emphasized there is nothing inevitable or guaranteed about growth. It also tends to bring retaliation. China has begun to experience problems of investment. Some countries, taking their cue from the USA, which has become very concerned about American companies that China either owns or has the majority shareholding in, have begun to block Chinese investment. But above all there is the political aspect to consider. The reason why China has taken such strides is that it has a huge manpower resource, and very low overheads, since Chinese workers are very poorly paid. It also has relatively low welfare costs. It is hard not to think that as China develops it will experience the problems that all modernizing states have undergone. Its workers will not put up indefinitely with small returns. The history of the workforce in every industrialized country is that workers begin to make unstoppable demands for a larger and fairer slice of the cake. There is no logical reason to think that China can avoid that process.

Problems of credit

In the second quarter of 2006 the Chinese economy grew at the rate of 11.3 per cent. Industrial output surged by nearly 18 per cent in the same period. At face value this is highly impressive, but there is a fear among Chinese financial experts, one shared by foreign observers, that China may be creating a bubble, and bubbles have a habit of bursting. The examples are the USA in 1929 and Japan in the 1980s. In those two countries a period of very rapid expansion, that gave rise to great optimism, suddenly came to a halt followed by a depression with very serious economic and social consequences. In the first half of 2006, China's state-run banks loaned the equivalent of over £250 billion to companies building factories and properties. The big question is whether that credit is recoverable. Standard & Poor, an international finance consultancy that monitors the fluctuations in world and national markets, calculates that China's 170,000 state-funded enterprises have accumulated 'bad debts' of over £800 million; that is another way of saying that they have been advanced money to that amount that they are unlikely to be able to pay back. In the event of a crisis, this could have a disastrous impact on China's whole financial system.

Problems of expansion

Odd though it sounds, China has been too successful in developing its export markets. The great economic strides it has made have been largely based on its ability to sell its goods abroad. But this has not been matched by a growth in its domestic market. Should there be a major falling off in its exports there is not the purchasing power within China to make up for the shortfall. While some Chinese have obviously become very wealthy, they are not a big enough proportion of the population to sustain a sales drive within China itself. As things stand in the first decade of the century, most Chinese simply do not earn enough to make China a consumer society on the scale necessary. A falling off in demand for China's manufactured goods is always a possibility.

It could come for a number of reasons. A recession among the developed countries could severely limit their power or wish to buy from China. A more politically motivated factor might be the rise of protectionism. Other countries might decide that the purchasing of Chinese goods damages their own domestic industries and therefore they will restrict Chinese imports. One example of this was the EU's decision in 2006 to limit imports of clothing and footwear from China. Another was the development of a strong protectionist bloc in the United States Congress dedicated to keeping Chinese goods out of America and allowing hard-pressed manufacturers to recover in the home market. If, for whatever reason, protectionism was to be widely applied internationally China would find it very difficult to avoid recession. The hard reality is that no single country is ever entirely in control of its own economy. It is always going to be affected by international trends and movements.

China's modern trauma

There is a sense in which China has been trapped by its own success. The new era of industrialization that began as a genuine desire to end poverty is now creating that very thing. Some

Chinese, principally those in the towns, have been able to adjust and have benefited enormously from industrial growth. But for many Chinese who do not have the resources or, equally importantly the mental attitude, to enable them to adjust, the results have been destructively disorientating. The pace of change is quicker than anything experienced by the Western nations. Developments have taken place in China in barely two generations that took centuries to occur in the other countries. Industrial revolutions have always brought difficulties in their wake but in most countries there has been time to adjust to the changes in society and ways of life that industry demands.

China simply has not had that time. This has produced a huge cultural shock. Growth on the scale being experienced runs counter to Chinese tradition. A century ago, China could be described as an unchanging society; there was a timelessness about it. It lacked the sense of progress that had influenced so many advanced countries, including its neighbour Japan. Yet during the next century it was wrenched by a series of crises and revolutions into the modern world. These were invariably hugely damaging to the ways and customs of ordinary Chinese: the fall of the Qing, the warlord savageries, the disruption of a long civil war, the corrupt rule of the Nationalists, the brutalities of the Japanese occupation, the misery of the Great Leap Forward and terrible famine that followed, the furious madness of the Cultural Revolution, and now an extraordinary and bewildering industrial revolution. Yet in none of this is there a consistent moral purpose. So many things seem arbitrary.

Education in China

In imperial China education was an exclusive affair, limited to the training of a governmental élite. The twentieth-century revolutionaries demanded that everyone was entitled to an education. Mao took this up when he was in power but what he sought was education for the masses, what might be described more accurately as mass indoctrination. This became violently clear during the Cultural Revolution when the schools and universities were closed and the students became the vanguard of the movement to smash the four olds that Mao had identified as the enemies of revolutionary progress. This disruptive nonsense was abandoned in the post-Mao era when Deng Xiaoping made education one of his four modernizations. His approach was essentially practical; he wanted China's brightest young people trained to be the planners, scientists and managers of the nation's move into industrial modernity. This resulted in the PRC paying relatively little attention to the idea of state education for all. The government claimed that shortage of money required that it give priority to the training of those best equipped to provide immediate service to the nation once they had qualified. This caused resentment among students who saw the education system as a corrupt method for extending privileges to party members. The student reaction culminated in what proved to be the tragic occupation of Tiananmen Square in 1989.

In the 1990s the students tended to lose their political edge; they became much more concerned with the practical question of preparing themselves to compete in the job market. State education at last began to spread. By 2000, the government claimed that 98 per cent of China's children were receiving a school education. It was in 2000 that the government set the target to be achieved within the decade of having 15 per cent of each year's school leavers enter higher education. This aim was close to being achieved by 2006. But even so, the demand for university admission was far greater than the places available.

China has 1,800 state universities and 1,300 technical colleges. Competition for university admission is intense. The basic entry requirement is the *gaokao*. This corresponds roughly to the English A level, but whereas over the last 20 years the English exam has been made progressively easier, its Chinese counterpart has been made progressively harder. Each year it is taken by 8 million 18-plus Chinese, 3 million of whom fail. A key reason is that to pass candidates, whatever their specialism, have to gain the equivalent of at least B in maths. The view among Chinese educationists is that in the modern China numeracy is as vital as literacy. Around 60 per cent of China's students study science subjects, which compares with only 35 per cent in Britain.

Surprisingly perhaps for a Communist society, education is no longer free for most Chinese. This is certainly true of higher education where students depend on parents, extended family and even the local community to pay their tuition fees and living costs. The Communist Party also funds the education of its members' children. Better-off students have a choice. They can either go abroad to university in Europe or the USA or they can attend one of the top universities in China where the equivalent of an ivy-league or Oxbridge system is developing. The United

Kingdom has a strong vested interest in Chinese students making the first of these choices. In 2006, for example, some 60,000 Chinese came to study at British universities. Since the fees paid by foreign students are much higher than those for British entrants, UK universities are very eager to recruit students from China.

Concerned that it was losing out in this way, Communist China made a major effort not only to retain its own students but to reverse the trend by encouraging foreign students to study in China. So strong had the reputation of China's most prestigious universities grown that by the mid-2000s there were more overseas students going to universities in China than there were Chinese students going abroad.

It was to keep a key place in the international higher-education market that some British universities, most notably Nottingham and Liverpool, took the battle to China itself. In 2005 Nottingham University opened an outpost in Shanghai. Boasting a staff of 60 British academics, it offered a range of degree courses, all taught in the English language. The fees charged were ten times dearer than those paid by Chinese students in their own universities. However, the attraction to Chinese parents was that the cost was a great deal lower than the expense involved in sending their children to study abroad.

What worries many Chinese is that, as is happening in other key areas of life, these developments in the universities threaten to destroy Communism's egalitarian principle by dividing China into two nations. Those who can afford to be educated will form a political and economic élite, which will have in-built advantages over the mass of the Chinese people. There is also a sense of disappointment that China's universities are still subject to government control of their administration and courses. Academic freedom has yet to come to China, and as long as the Communist authorities continue to claim an absolute right to dictate social policy it is difficult to see how it could come.

The gender issue is also important. Despite the spread of formal education for females, it is they who tend to miss out. There is still a prejudice against women being educated. This is because education is not free in China. Since it has to be paid for by the family, it is invariably the boys' education into which the parents and grandparents put their savings. There is also the lingering tradition that a girl on marriage becomes part of her husband's household so there is little likelihood of her contributing to her own family after that. Naturally, therefore, parents opt to spend on their son in the hope that when they are old he will provide for them. It is an attitude of mind that may take some time to change.

Preparing for the Beijing Games, 2008

The year 2008 will provide China with an opportunity as never before to show its face to the world. Sadly, the preparations for the Olympics have already shown an aspect of modern China that the Chinese are anxious for the world not to see. The stadium being built in Beijing for the athletic events and the opening and closing ceremonies will accommodate 100,000 spectators; covering an area of 30,000 square feet it will be the largest enclosed space on earth. It is magnificent but deadly. So desperate is Beijing to be ready for the Games that it has asked its workers to be prepared to die for it. This is not a figure of speech. In the summer of 2006, on the scaffolding of the rising stadium were hung banners and placards urging the workers to ever greater efforts. One of the placards reads, 'the Quality of Work is more important than Life'. When foreign journalists made their guided visit to the site such placards were covered up or taken down.

The managers of the company building the stadium claimed there had been no deaths or even serious injuries. But even the government's own Construction Ministry admitted to 50 deaths on site in the first half of 2006; independent labour organizations, not under direct government control, suggest that the number can be at least doubled to give a truer picture. A major problem is that proper accident records are not kept. According to the *Labour Bulletin*, published privately in Hong Kong, 'only between 5 and 10 per cent of work place accidents are officially reported'. The Asia Monitor Resource Centre reports 'injured or fatally wounded workers are simply removed to keep the figures tidy'. The International Labour Office calculates that 26 per cent of the world's on-site fatal accidents among construction workers occur in China.

The 2,000 or so who were employed building the stadium in Beijing were mainly migrants from the countryside who were willing to work for minimum wages in unprotected conditions. They were billeted on site in sweltering pre-fabricated huts that served as living quarters and dormitories with three or four bunks rising on either side of a narrow aisle. Their weekly pay was 250 yuan (£17). Alerted by whispers of what was really happening, the Construction Ministry in 2006 made a great show of setting safety standards. A 'People's Supervision Project' was announced and guide books were distributed explaining basic safety rules to the workers and how they could claim compensation. But all this was largely propaganda, meant to impress the public rather than genuinely assist the workers. For one thing, the cost of making a claim was invariably greater than the amount of compensation awarded; for another, few of the workers had sufficient understanding of urban ways to know what a claim was.

One of the 2,000 workers who did not survive long enough to make a claim was Chen Zulin, a migrant from Sichuan province. In February 2006, he was 200 feet up in a cradle painting one of the five Olympic rings; it was the green one. The brush slipped from his hand. The quick movement he made to catch it tilted the cradle forward. He was not wearing a harness. Chen fell to the ground and was killed instantly.

Water

Beijing's scramble to be ready for the Games has also highlighted one of China's greatest needs – water. Its shortage of water presents it with gargantuan problems. It is trying gargantuan answers. The Three Gorges Project was one of these. Another is the 'south–north canals', a plan that will take until mid-century to complete at an estimated cost of £30 to £40 billion, which is twice that of the Three Gorges. The aim is to link four major rivers, the Yellow, the Yangzi, the Huaihe and the Haihe, in transferring 45 billion cubic tons of water every year to northern and eastern China.

The scheme envisages the construction of three main canals which, drawing their water from the four main rivers, will extend hundreds of miles over ground by means of giant aqueducts and under ground through great tunnels. Two sections of tunnelling had already been completed by 2006; these were in Hebei province and will eventually connect with Beijing's Grand Canal, constructed by slave labour over two and a half millennia ago. This section was given precedence in order to guarantee adequate water supplies to the capital in time for the Olympics.

The big question relates not to financial but to environmental costs. Chinese and foreign conservations are warning that the canals may destroy far more than ever they create. Half a

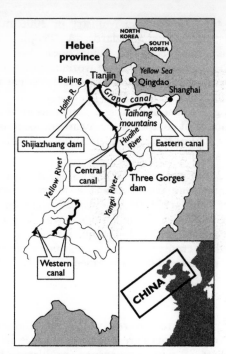

figure 11 South–North construction scheme

million Chinese will have to be relocated, flora and fauna will be obliterated, and pollution will proliferate as natural tributary waterways are diverted and also used as great dumping areas. The government has rejected all counter arguments and insists that pollution will not occur on a significant scale. Its position, on which it has said it will not budge, is that since the less-populated southern and western provinces of China have 81 per cent of China's water it makes perfect sense that part of this should be redirected to the populous areas of the north where water need is becoming desperate. It is a matter of fairness and necessity. That is the government's reasoning. It is all part of the economic and social revolution to which the People's Republic of China has committed itself.

15

China at the crossroads

This chapter will cover:
- China's human rights record
- its policy of suppression
- China's options for the future.

China's violation of human rights

One of the greatest barriers to China's march to modernity is its government's refusal to extend political and civil rights to its people. The annual reports by the various world bodies monitoring human rights in China do not make attractive reading. It is a grim story of the disregard of internationally agreed standards which China has formally accepted, having signed up to both the Universal Declaration on Human Rights and the International Covenant on Civil and Political Rights. Basic to the PRC's repression is the conviction that it is improper for its citizens to challenge its authority. The right to seek to change the government or the Communist system is simply not recognized. Those who openly express opposition can expect to be arrested and imprisoned. This applies as much to those whose challenge is based on religious or nationalist grounds as it does to those whose dissent is political. The need for state security is always given as the reason for the authorities' intolerance of opposition, regardless of the motivation behind it. In July 2003, the government restated its position very clearly by issuing 'The Three Forbiddens', topics that the people must not discuss. These were constitutional reform, political reform, and the 1989 Tiananmen Square demonstration.

The PRC's codes of law read as if they offered full protection to the citizen from oppressive government. But the codes read better than they operate. It is extremely difficult and very rare for ordinary citizens to gain redress. Officials simply do not admit to serious errors; besides which the legal system is not independent. It is dominated by the government; judges and magistrates are Communist Party appointees and see their role as upholding the rule of the party in China. A woman judge in Beijing, admitted without qualm: 'I am a judge. At the same time I am also a Communist Party member. I must do my duty. All positions in the court are controlled by the Communist Party so it is impossible for the courts to be free from the control of the party.'

This is why reported cases of ill treatment of state prisoners are seldom inquired into; torture, forced confessions and deaths while in custody continue year by year. China has no equivalent of the *habeas corpus* principle, so arrests and detention without charge are common practice. Even when judicial review of cases is promised, this seldom happens. In January 2003, a Tibetan independence activist, Lobsang Dondrub, was executed the day after the authorities, in response to appeals from abroad, had said they would send his case for re-consideration to the Chinese Supreme People's Court.

The 'strike hard' campaign

In 2001, to great fanfares, the Chinese government announced that it was implementing a nationwide 'strike hard' campaign against crime. The aim, it was officially stated, was to provide greater social order and give the people better protection against 'criminal elements'. Beijing witnessed the execution of 13,000 prisoners after they had been publicly paraded through the streets. The real purpose of the campaign was to provide a cover for even more severe measures to be taken against the independence movements in the western provinces. Tibet and Xinjiang were specially targeted; mass public trials and executions became a common sight. Beijing claimed that 'three evils' had to be eradicated in the two provinces. These were defined as 'ethnic separatism, illegal religious activities, and violent terrorism'. By grouping the three together, terrorism with religion and the independence movement, the authorities gave themselves a free hand to crush political and religious dissent under the banner of fighting crime.

The laogai

In 2005 there were 300,000 known cases of prisoners held in 're-education-through-labour' camps with no chance of their appealing successfully for release or shorter sentences. It was in one of these camps that a prisoner, Zhang Bin, was battered to death by fellow inmates. It later leaked out that although Zhang was a political prisoner the guards had deliberately put him unprotected in a section reserved for the most violent criminals. Ex-prisoners have reported that the guards often take sadistic pleasure from punishing political prisoners, dubbed 'intellectuals', in this fashion.

For obvious reasons, the government does not provide figures for the total number of prisoners held officially or unofficially in China, but observers calculate that the overall number, including state prisons and labour camps, is between 3 and 4 million. One estimate that deserves attention is that of Harry Wu, who spent 20 years as a prisoner in various parts of the laogai, the collective term for the whole camp system. Writing in the late 1990s, he asserted that there were 1,155 camps, holding between them some 6 to 8 million prisoners. 'The world knows that perhaps a few people were killed at Tiananmen Square in 1989. I say that incident was peanuts. One way or another, millions of people have been lost in the laogai.'

It is in the 're-education-through-labour' camps that the worst conditions are to be found. Starvation and overwork are an integral part of the regime. It is in these camps that, under slave-labour conditions, so many of the items are made, like key-rings, cigarette lighters and Christmas decorations, which the Western world buys in their millions. There is a cruel cynicism in the title of the camps. Communist thinking deems that for anyone to commit a crime, whether anti-social or political, means that he has not fully grasped the enlightened character of the society he is living in. The purpose of the imprisonment, is not, therefore, to punish him but to re-educate him into a true understanding of Communist ways. Once he has discovered this he will no longer wish to be a criminal. There are labour camps for females where the women know that the more lustily and enthusiastically they sing the camp songs that tell of the joys of Chinese Communism the more chance they have of parole or reduction of their sentence.

Crimes and misdemeanours

Every society has its thieves, rapists and murderers. But in China it is not these but the political dissidents and the protesters against corruption and pollution who are disproportionately punished. Yang Jianli who spoke out for greater political freedoms was arrested in 2003 and held without charge. Even though the UN Working Group on Arbitrary Detention pleaded his cause with the Chinese government and stressed that his detention contravened the letter and spirit of the Human Rights Convention that China has signed, he was still in prison two years later. What in most countries would be regarded as legitimate protest is prohibited in China. When, for example, in 2003, a group of workers demonstrated against their employers for not paying their wages, the government stepped in, had the workers' leaders, Yao Fuxin and Xiao Yunliang, arrested and given lengthy prison sentences for 'state subversion'.

It was also in 2003 that Zheng Enchong was imprisoned not for a specific crime but for acting as the representative of a group of low-income residents who had been ejected from their homes in Shanghai to make way for an urban redevelopment scheme. In Henan province, Ma Shiwen, a welfare officer, was arrested for 'revealing state secrets'; the offence consisted of having told the truth about the way thousands of patients had contracted HIV after an administrative error had led to their receiving contaminated blood. Since the persecution of Falun Gong began in 1999, thousands of the movement's members have been imprisoned, many hundreds of these dying from deliberate ill treatment. In September of the same year, the High Court of Shaanxi province rejected a request from prisoner Ma Wenlin, a lawyer, to have his original conviction reviewed. He had been found guilty of 'disturbing social order'. His crime was to have represented a group of peasants in an appeal they had made to have their taxes cut.

A depressing feature of Chinese legal processes is that 90 per cent of all cases end in verdicts of guilty, which means that the hearings are not really trials but rather procedures to justify the sentences that are then handed out. An example of this injustice was the fate of Tao Haidong, a political campaigner in Urumqi in Xinjiang province, who was charged with 'incitement to subvert state power', a reference to his having set up web pages calling for democracy. He was told long before he went into court that he would be found guilty and made an example of by being given a seven-year gaol term. He was.

The death penalty

One of the major complaints against China from human rights campaigners is that not only does it retain capital punishment but that it uses it as a regular penalty rather than one of a last resort. There are currently 65 offences for which capital punishment is the penalty; these include forgery, embezzlement, and corruption. On the PRC government's own admission, between 2000 and 2005 an average of 15,000 prisoners were executed every year. One of the grimmest features in the process is the practice of sending the family of the executed the bullet that killed him along with a bill for the cost of it. Chinese officials struggle to deny stories that the organs of executed prisoners are routinely extracted and sold for transplant.

The case of Chen Guangcheng

The abuse to which dissidents of simple seekers after justice in China are subjected is typified by the case of Chen Guangcheng. Chen, a lawyer who happens to be blind, for years ran a personal campaign to expose government and party officials who had abused their authority by using bribery and intimidation. Known as the 'barefoot lawyer', since like the barefoot doctors he often gave his services freely to ordinary Chinese who were being prosecuted by the authorities, Chen was placed under house arrest in August 2005. His crime was that he had tried to bring an action against the officials in the family planning department of the Shandong provincial government for buying and selling birth permits. He also produced evidence showing that over 7,000 women in the province had suffered enforced abortions and sterilization. Groups of officials, police and civilians keen to gain favour from the authorities, sometimes numbering as many as 300 in all, surrounded his house. Fellow lawyers who came from Beijing to give Chen moral support were denied entry to his home, beaten by the police and arrested. In March 2006 Chen was dragged from his house and taken to a detention centre for interrogation where he was told, 'Nobody minds if someone dies while in here.'

The authorities initially denied that he was in custody but eventually, when details appeared on a web site revealing that he had 'disappeared', admitted that they held him. Lawyers who still attempted to help Chen were either refused permission to see him or allowed so little time with him that they could not prepare an adequate defence case. In June it was announced that Chen would be formally tried at the end of July. In the interim, hired thugs terrorized Chen's family, including his 70-year-old mother and three-year-old son, and physically attacked lawyers still courageous enough to be willing to defend him openly.

In August 2006, after a trial described by a fellow dissident Hu Jia as 'completely illegal from the beginning', Chen was given a four-year prison sentence. The charge on which he was convicted was that he had acted 'with intent to damage public property and inciting others to join him to disrupt traffic'. Sophie Richardson, a director of the Asia Human Rights Watch, explained the significance of Chen Guangcheng's case: 'When Cheng tried to make proper use of China's legal system, the response wasn't due process. It was house arrest, physical abuse, and then 'disappearance' by local authorities. His case is a textbook example of how little the rule of law really means in China.'

The case of Zhao Yan

A similar disregard for legal processes was apparent in the case of Zhao Yan, a Chinese assistant at the *New York Times* office in Beijing. In 2004 he dared to inform his paper of a row between President Hu Jintao and ex-President Jiang Zemin over senior appointments in the Chinese armed services. Zhao's information, which the *New York Times* published, was wholly accurate; there had been a dispute and Jiang Zemin had resigned as a result of it. Nevertheless, Zhao was seized by the authorities for having 'revealed state secrets to a foreign power'. He was held in custody without formal charge, his family were refused access to him and threatened, and his lawyer was continually harassed. Eventually, after facing many protests from international freedom campaigners, a trial date was set for June 2006, but the prosecutors announced sternly that it was a wholly Chinese domestic matter and they would not take any lectures or criticisms from foreign representatives.

Suppression of women's rights

A particular point made by human rights watchers is that despite the PRC's constitution, which guarantees protection and equality for women, it is often females whose rights are trampled on by the state. One example is the violence against women that, under the government's birth limitation policies, takes the form of enforced abortions and compulsory sterilization. It is still possible for women to be imprisoned simply by the decision of the local police. There is a so-called 'model' women's prison outside Beijing where the majority of prisoners are serving sentences for having caused 'social disturbances', being involved in prostitution or drug selling. On the word of a police officer, they are simply incarcerated without a trial or a chance to defend themselves.

The Chinese have been very defensive over women's rights ever since the 1990s when it was claimed in the West in a number of books and television documentaries that female babies were being deliberately neglected and left to die in China's orphanages. The PRC's response then was to condemn the stories as malicious anti-Chinese rumour mongering. And it was true that the evidence did not support the idea of a systematic attempt by the PRC to kill its girl babies. But a balanced conclusion might be that although there was no planned infanticide, there was certainly widespread abuse and ill treatment of young girls in the orphanages. This was, in part at least, a consequence of modern China's population control policies.

The scale of government control

Many Chinese, even politically progressive ones, are sometimes heard suggesting that perhaps the government's ban on discussing the Tiananmen Square incident is no bad thing. Maybe it is time to forgive and forget the massacre of 1989. It happened so long ago; better to draw a veil over it, and make a fresh start. This seems a reasonable suggestion until one looks at some figures. In 2005, 17 years after that event, there were around 2,000 people still in prison who had been arrested after their demonstration had been crushed. In May 2004, a web site manager in Sichuan was given a five-year prison sentence for setting up a site where people could look for relatives who had disappeared after the 1989 Tiananmen tragedy. Not much forgiving and forgetting there.

To indicate just how widely the government's grip on Chinese society extends, it is worth listing a sample of those currently imprisoned in the PRC for political crimes. The list might also serve as a small tribute to a set of very brave people. Wang Youcai and Qin Yongmin, founders of the banned Chinese Democratic Party; Xu Wei, Yang Zili and Huang Qi, who have used the internet as a vehicle for expressing free ideas; Rebiya Kadeer, a Uighur businesswoman who spoke out against PRC repression in Xinjiang; Jiang Weiping, a journalist who would not be deterred from writing things the government found unpalatable; Yao Fuxin, Xiao Yunliang, and Liu Jingsheng, who fought for workers' rights; Bishop Su Zhimin, who told the authorities not to oppress his Catholic flock; Zhang Yinan, Liu Fenggang and Xu Yonghai, who led the house church movement; Phuntsog Nyidrol, a Tibetan nun, who stood up for her native faith and culture; Tohti Tunyaz, a Uighur historian, who saw it as his duty to write truth not government propaganda. All these people have become the special concern of international human rights groups.

Government attitudes towards homosexual rights

By tradition, the Chinese Communist Party was suspicious of the idea of rights for homosexuals. As with religion, it was unhappy with a movement whose sense of community might undermine its commitment to the brotherhood of Communism. However, in 2001, the government-sponsored China Psychiatric Association took homosexuality off its list of mental illnesses. Would this lead to greater official tolerance? The omens seemed good until, in December 2005, police moved in to break up the Beijing Gay and Lesbian Culture Festival, the first event of its kind held in the PRC. The organizers interpreted the police action as indicating that the Communist authorities had not abandoned their old attitudes. The regret was not simply over the question of civil rights. One of the claims made by the gay movement was that it had done a great deal to make the Chinese aware of the AIDS epidemic and how it might be tackled. If homosexuals were now to be debarred from contributing to the debate, the government's programme for combating the disease would be badly damaged.

Psychiatry as repression

For many years one of the major suspicions about the PRC was that it was misusing psychiatry as a weapon of political control. It was suspected that dissidents and those who asked awkward questions were being classified as mentally disturbed rather than criminal, which meant their views could be dismissed as nonsense and they could be shut away in mental institutions indefinitely. There were reports that many of the members of the Falun Gong who were arrested were shut up in such places. It was a scandal that brought condemnation from the world's professional psychiatrists. Matters were highlighted in March 2006 when Wang Wanxing, who for 13 years had been forcibly detained in an 'ankang', a psychiatric hospital for the criminally insane, was finally released and went to Holland. There he was examined by a team of Dutch doctors who declared him totally sane. It was the clearest evidence yet of China's lack of scruples in dealing with political opposition. In the words of the director of Asian Human Rights Watch, 'The conclusion of the expert team confirms our long-held suspicions. China has been repeatedly accused of using psychiatry as a tool of political repression, but until Wang left China, it was impossible to verify the accusations.'

Chinese reaction to criticism of its record

The Chinese are highly touchy on this. They do not easily take criticism. It is not part of the Chinese temperament. To acknowledge criticism is to admit guilt. This was why the self-criticism sessions had been such a terrifying feature of the Maoist era. They claim that they are vilified by anti-Chinese bodies who, backed by the Americans, try to paint as black a picture as possible. They also stress that China has its own human rights organizations such as the China Society for Human Rights Studies, but since this body talks only on the supposed advances being made and does not tackle the questions put to it by the international community it is difficult to see it as other than a government mouthpiece.

Nevertheless in an attempt to clear itself and embarrass the USA, the PRC retaliated in kind in March 2005 by publishing, in the same solemn form as the annual American reports on China, its own report on the USA. The tone of the report can be gauged from its opening sentence: 'American society is characterized with rampant violent crimes, severe infringement of people's rights by law enforcement departments and lack of guarantee for people's rights to life, liberty and security of person.'

Western responses

Periodically major figures in Britain have been criticized in parliament and the media for their lack of urgency in criticizing China's poor human rights record. Margaret Thatcher was censured in 1990 for allowing a formal visit of a PRC delegation while at the same time refusing to grant the Dalai Lama an official visit. Although she sympathized with the Tibetan leader's position, she claimed it would be imprudent to allow him to visit Britain in an official capacity as this might upset the Chinese with whom Britain was conducting delicate negotiations over trade and commerce. In 1999 Tony Blair's government was attacked in parliament for not only entertaining a Chinese delegation led by Jiang Zemin but also for ordering the Metropolitan Police to break up demonstrations by groups of Tibetan sympathizers and force them down side roads so they could not be seen and therefore be an embarrassment to the official Chinese delegation. Many argued this was both a betrayal of the Tibetan human rights movement and totally contrary to the British tradition of legitimate protest.

Ken Livingstone, the Mayor of London, rather damaged his democratic credentials when, on a visit to Beijing in 2005 to study Chinese preparations for the 2008 Olympic Games, he made a number of statements that suggested his sympathies lay with the Chinese government and that he was unwilling, openly at least, to protest against human rights violations in China. His answer, and it is one often heard from officials who are caught up in this issue, was that there was more chance of influencing the Chinese leaders in private talks than by making open challenges which, given the sensitivity of the Chinese in this area, would most likely result in their refusing to talk further. In other words, formal attacks upon China will not get very far and will only create ill will, while informal contacts may make a great deal more progress. This is a reasonable argument but its weakness is that it lets the Chinese leaders off the hook. In private they could agree to anything put to them and make promises to recognize human rights, but since no formal commitment is required of them they could not then be held to account.

It is noteworthy that it is not merely Western governments who kow-tow to Beijing. In June 2006, the South Korean government earned the anger of libertarians when it refused to grant a visa to the Dalai Lama that would have allowed him to attend a gathering of Nobel Prize winners in Gwangju. The government's explanation was that his visit would not be 'desirable', a lame way of saying that South Korea did not wish to upset the Chinese.

Can China cope with modernity?

China is a country with massive potential. The big question is whether it can overcome its internal contradictions and realize that potential by developing as a democratic fully modernized state. It could, of course, be objected that the PRC's success should not be judged by a democratic standard that, after all, is a Western way of approaching things. It may settle for stability and order. But those, too, are under threat. There are religious and separatist forces that, although under control at present, may yet prove too strong and bring about disruption if not disintegration. It has not helped that, since Deng Xiaoping, China's leaders have been a pretty nondescript bunch, party functionaries rather than inspirational national figures.

There is a fear, even among pro-government Chinese, that the PRC faces huge internal threats. There are predictions that if the gap between urban workers and rural peasants goes on widening, and the government still forbids the expression of dissent, the result could be an outburst of frustration far more serious than in 1989. David Zweig, a Hong Kong economist, dramatically asks, 'There are hundreds of little brush fires burning. Will they become a blaze?' Modern China was born in violence and has been sustained by it. It is a country that, arguably, has modernized too suddenly and when it finds it cannot cope with that degree of change it may revert to violence.

The problem will be that as China advances pressure at ground level will begin to build. But can a society that has for the overwhelming part of its existence been authoritarian and conformist adjust? The party will not let go the levers of power. The 6 per cent of the population who are members of the ruling CCP party are not about to relinquish their privileges.

Mao's lingering presence

How China will develop only the future can tell, but we can make the attempt to understand China as it stands. In a number of respects Mao's China still operates. His economics have been abandoned, but the PRC remains committed to Marxism. It is a one-party state. This is important not simply in governmental or political terms. The Communist Party is the great dispenser of patronage. Jobs, salaries, career prospects, education, access to food are all within the party's gift. A Chinese citizen who is not a party member is effectively powerless.

Does Chinese democracy have a future?

It is realistic to be sceptical about the prospects for democracy in China. There is no great democratic movement in China today. Tiananmen Square 1989 may indeed prove to be the isolated aberration that Deng Xiaoping at the time said it was. Some of the brightest young people have become dissidents, sometimes fleeing abroad, but a far greater majority of the nation's most able have stayed. True, they might complain about individual aspects of the Communist system but they do not doubt its basic value to them as a promotional ladder. As an aspiring young Chinese lawyer said at a British Council soirée in Beijing in 2006, 'The British system would not work here. I think the one-party state is good for China right now. We must join the Communist Party and work for the government. It is a great honour to join the party. You must be a very bright student.'

What this suggests is that the Chinese protest movement has been beheaded. The most talented of China's young have been bought off and recruited for the party. Opposition is now rarely to be found among the ranks of the intellectuals and the high-flyers. Where protest is to be found it is among the dissatisfied workers and persecuted religious minorities. But these groups are unco-ordinated and ill-organized. As was shown in 2005, when there was a rash of demonstrations among Christians, Muslims and Buddhists against state interference, the government had little trouble in dispersing the protesters and then portraying them as enemies of the State.

Adjusting to the new

It may also be that the young are not disorientated in the way their elders have been. They may settle happily for the brash new China typified by the garish and raucous advertising that is now everywhere in China's cities. Until recent times Chinese advertising often combined subtlety and self-abasement. For example, Shanghai's well-known restauranteur, Chuh Fong, would not boast how wonderful his food and service were. Instead he would say something along the lines of: 'Unworthy though he is, Chuh Fong invites you to grace him with your honoured presence in his humble eating house.' Not for him the strident drum-beating of a McDonald's or Kentucky Fried Chicken. His object was the same as theirs of course, to part the customers from their money, but there was a touch of refinement about it. This has largely gone. With the quickening pace of life, China wants fast food outlets, not traditional banquets and prolonged meals. One unsought for but inevitable result is that the Chinese are putting on weight. Already there are worrying signs that China's children are becoming obese. The one-child policy has led parents and grandparents to over-indulge their one little darling by overfeeding him. Young boys have begun to take on the shape of the Buddha whose image the PRC has put so much energy into trying to destroy.

Worker revolt?

Speculations about China's economic future often take an optimistic line by suggesting that China will become one of the giants of the twenty-first century. There are also sceptics, however, who suggest that China's modernity is a veneer and that behind it all is a nation that does not really understand, even if it appears to want, the apparatus of modern stock markets and international finance. Communist China has been described as a bandit society, based not on defensible social principles but on bribery and threats, money laundering by venal élites and political corruption.

When its bluff is called perhaps it will all collapse. If China follows the pattern experienced by all societies that have modernized, there will soon come a time when workers will rebel against their exploitation. As the producers of wealth, they will begin to demand a larger slice of the cake. When that happens certain consequences are likely to follow. If the workers' demands are accepted, wages will rise and profits will fall. This will decrease China's competitiveness. If the workers' claims are rejected, frustration will mount; since China's authoritarian regime does not tolerate protest the consequence is likely to be increased repression. There might then be a revolution from below on a scale to match those that have made China tremble in times past.

China's modern character

China emerged into the twenty-first century as a strange amalgam of the traditional and the revolutionary. In the first decade of the new millennium China is struggling to reconcile many of its old values, which somehow survived recent systematic attempts to destroy them, with the demands of the new. There is little doubt that China wants to be a truly modern nation. It has embarked on an extraordinary programme of capitalist industrial and commercial development. Yet all this is presided over by a Communist government that until a generation ago was sworn to the annihilation of capitalism. One wonders for how long China's one party regime can successfully maintain this paradox. It defies logic to expect that an authoritarian government committed to a policy of total political control can keep its ideology permanently in balance with its contradictory economic policy. Experience suggests that something has got to give.

The Chinese imperial system collapsed in 1911 because it was in crisis. The doubling of China's population within a century, and the subjection of China to foreign control during that time had subjected its major institutions, the law, government and administration, to pressures that proved unendurable. The system broke into pieces. The question is whether 100 years later, the pressures on Communist China might not prove equally unbearable.

Zhou Enlai was asked in 1953 what he thought was the greatest change brought by the French Revolution of the eighteenth century. He replied that it was too early to tell. If a future Zhou were to be asked what changes the Chinese revolution had wrought he might have a rather shorter timescale to work with.

glossary

AWACS Airborne Warning and Control System

Dalai Lama The spiritual leader of Tibet's Lama faith.

Dangan A dossier compiled by the PRC government, containing details of all politically suspect persons in China.

De lai Sui 'Come and get it fast', the name of a projected McDonalds in Beijing.

Détente A policy aimed at easing relations between the Eastern bloc and Western nations by encouraging mutual acceptance of co-existence.

Falun Gong A modern religion belonging to the Taoist–Buddhist tradition; it holds that mind and body are one and are best developed by spiritual and physical exercises.

Four Cardinal Principles Defined by Deng Xiaoping as: keeping to the socialist road, upholding the people's democratic dictatorship, upholding leadership by the Communist Party and upholding Marxism–Leninism and Mao Zedong thought.

Four modernizations Deng Xiaoping's basic reform programme: the reform of agriculture, industry, defence and education.

Four olds Old ideas, old culture, old customs, old habits – the targets selected by Mao for attack during the Cultural Revolution.

Gaokao Chinese university entry requirement, roughly equivalent to A level.

Historical determinism The notion that events do not happen haphazardly but are part of a preordained pattern of development.

Hutong These were grey stone alleyways that linked the tiny one-level houses in which most ordinary Beijingers used to live, but which are now being demolished.

Iron rice bowl The system that developed under Mao which provided workers with a guaranteed job and wages.

Khampas The traditional nomadic herdsmen of Tibet.

Kyoto Protocol The international agreement, signed in 1997, to limit the emission of greenhouse gases.

Laogai The Chinese prison and labour camp system, which began under Mao and still operates today.

LEGCO The Legislative Council of Hong Kong.

Little Red Book The popular name for *Quotations from Chairman Mao Tse-tung*, the book which became the bible of Maoist China.

Oligarchy Rule by a privileged group.

Panchen Lama The Dalai Lama's deputy.

PLA The People's Liberation Army (formerly the Red Army).

Revisionism A Marxist term applied to those Communists who were willing to compromise with capitalism and the enemies of Communism.

San gang The Confucian three bonds that held society together – loyalty of officials to the emperor, obedience of wives to husband, respect of children for parents.

Sutras The sacred texts of the Tibetan Lama religion.

Three forbiddens A prohibition issued by the PRC in July 2003, forbidding the people to discuss: constitutional reform, political reform, and the 1989 Tiananmen Square demonstration.

Three Noes Issued by President Clinton in 1998: No to independent Taiwan, No to two Chinas, No to Taiwan being accepted as a member by international organizations.

Tiger economies The Asian regions, for example, Singapore, South Korea and Hong Kong, that flourished in the second half of the twentieth century.

Tsampa A paste made from Barley, a staple food of the Tibetans.

Unequal treaties Agreements imposed on China by foreign governments which left the Chinese disadvantaged.

Velvet Revolutions The popular uprisings in eastern Europe which began in 1989 and brought down all the Communist bloc governments.

Zhongguo The Chinese word for China meaning 'the Middle Kingdom'.

taking it further

Changes are occurring so rapidly in China that in one sense every book on it is out of date as soon as it is published. Nevertheless the following very selective list offers as up-to-date an analysis of events as is possible in the circumstances.

Jasper Becker, *Hungry Ghosts: China's Secret Famine* (John Murray 1996) – the first major study in English to reveal the truth concerning the terrible Mao-made famine that left such a fearful mark on China.

Hugo de Burgh, *China: Friend or Foe* (Icon, 2006) – offers many interesting thoughts on how the outside world should view China.

Gordon G. Chang, *The Coming Collapse of China* (Arrow Books, 2002) – a doom-laden analysis arguing that China cannot sustain itself as a modern industrial nation and that within a decade the communist government will have been brought down.

Jung Chang & Jon Halliday, *Mao the Unknown Story* (Jonathan Cape, 2005) – a very long and impassioned attack on Mao's reputation by the well-known Chinese writer whose family were persecuted during the Cultural Revolution. The following biographies, while far from sympathetic to Mao, provide more balanced (and much shorter) accounts of Mao's life and his impact on China: Delia Davin, *Mao Zedong* (Sutton, 1997); Lee Feigon, *Mao: a Reinterpretation* (Ivan R. Dee, 2002); Michael Lynch, *Mao* (Routledge, 2004); Jonathan Spence, *Mao* (Weidenfeld & Nicolson, 1999).

Harriet Evans, *Women and Sexuality in China* (Polity Press, 1997) – surveys the restrictions on, and opportunities for, women in China.

Richard Evans, *Deng Xiaoping and the Making of Modern China* (1991) – an informed account of new era reforms that laid the base for the growth of modern China.

John Gittings, *The Changing Face of China: From Mao to Market* (Oxford University Press, 2005) – traces the ways in which China has tried to unburden itself of the legacy of Mao and embrace modernity.

Doug Guthrie, *China and Globalization* (Routledge, 2006) – takes an optimistic line in suggesting that China will successfully modernize both economically and politically.

Palden Gyatso, *Fire Under the Snow* (Harvill 1997) – a moving account by one of its victims of China's suppression of Tibet.

Peter Hessler, *Oracle Bones: A Journey between China's Past and Present* (John Murray, 2006) – an absorbing attempt to relate current developments in China to its long history.

Graham Hutchings, *Modern China: A Companion to a Great Power* (Penguin, 2001) – a very useful reference book that keeps a nice balance between narrative and analysis.

Nicholas D. Kristof & Sheryl Wudunn, *China Wakes: the Struggle for the Soul of a Rising Power* (nb publishing, 1998) – a very lively, anecdotal treatment by two American journalists based in China.

James Kynge, *China Shakes the World: The Rise of a Hungry Nation* (Weidenfeld and Nicholson, 2006) – views the growth of China as an international threat.

Justin Yifu Lin, *The China Miracle* (Chinese University Press, 2006) – explores the extraordinary changes that have come upon China over the last generation.

Lydia H. Liu, *The Clash of Empires: the Invention of China in Modern World Making* (Harvard University Press, 2004) – puts modern China in its historical context.

Pamela C. M. Mar, *China Enabling a New Era of Changes* (John Wiley & Sons, 2003) – provides another insightful analysis of recent developments in China.

Edwin E. Moise, *Modern China: a History* (Longman, 2006) – one of the latest general introductions to modern China.

W. Scott Morton & Charlton M. Lewis, *China: its History and Culture* (McGraw-Hill, 2005) – analyses the ways of modern China through its history.

Peter Nolan, *China at the Crossroads* (Blackwell, 2005) – discusses the economic and political options open to China.

Kevin J. O'Brien & Jiang Jang Li, *Rightful Resistance in Rural China* (CUP, 2006) – deals with the movements that have arisen in reaction to the destructive changes in the Chinese countryside.

Tony Saich, *Governance and Politics of China* (Palgrave, 2004) – a masterly study of the way the Communist Party currently runs China.

Orville Schell, *Mandate of Heaven* (Time Warner, 1996) – a leading authority's provocative treatment of China's struggle to modernize.

Jonathan Spence and Annping Chin, *The Chinese Century, A Photographic History* (HarperCollins, 1996) – provides wonderful photographs and a brilliant commentary on China's juddering advance towards the new age.

Michael Schoenhals (Ed.), *China's Cultural Revolution, 1966–69* (M. E. Sharpe, 1996) – provides a fascinating set of documents on this central episode in modern Chinese history.

Ross Terrill, *The New Chinese Empire* (Basic Books, 2003) – examines Chinese ambitions and aspirations.

Wang Hui, *China's New Order* (Harvard University Press, 2003) – looks at the changing social and political structure of China.

Wei Jingsheng, *The Courage to Stand Alone* (Penguin, 1998) – a personal account of his struggles by the outstanding pro-democracy activist of the Deng era.

Dick Wilson, *China: the Big Tiger* (Little Brown, 1996) – a very lively account of China's effort to adapt to great power status.

Harry Wu, *Laogai – China's Gulag* (Chatto & Windus 1993) – details the brutal persecution of dissent in China by a leading Chinese activist.

Zhang Xianliang, *My Bodhi tree* (Secker 1996) – another disturbing account by a victim the PRC's political repression.

There are a number of helpful web pages on the internet. One to be especially recommended is BBC NEWS in depth China. The pages by Asia Watch and Amnesty International are also well worth consulting, as is the Chinese government's own official portal GOV.cn.

teach yourself®

From Advanced Sudoku to Zulu, you'll find everything you need in the **teach yourself** range, in books, on CD and on DVD.

Visit **www.teachyourself.co.uk** for more details.

Advanced Sudoku and Kakuro
Afrikaans
Alexander Technique
Algebra
Ancient Greek
Applied Psychology
Arabic
Aromatherapy
Art History
Astrology
Astronomy
AutoCAD 2004
AutoCAD 2007
Ayurveda
Baby Massage and Yoga
Baby Signing
Baby Sleep
Bach Flower Remedies
Backgammon
Ballroom Dancing
Basic Accounting
Basic Computer Skills
Basic Mathematics
Beauty
Beekeeping
Beginner's Arabic Script
Beginner's Chinese Script
Beginner's Dutch

Beginner's French
Beginner's German
Beginner's Greek
Beginner's Greek Script
Beginner's Hindi
Beginner's Italian
Beginner's Japanese
Beginner's Japanese Script
Beginner's Latin
Beginner's Mandarin Chinese
Beginner's Portuguese
Beginner's Russian
Beginner's Russian Script
Beginner's Spanish
Beginner's Turkish
Beginner's Urdu Script
Bengali
Better Bridge
Better Chess
Better Driving
Better Handwriting
Biblical Hebrew
Biology
Birdwatching
Blogging
Body Language
Book Keeping
Brazilian Portuguese

Bridge
British Empire, The
British Monarchy from Henry
  VIII, The
Buddhism
Bulgarian
Business Chinese
Business French
Business Japanese
Business Plans
Business Spanish
Business Studies
Buying a Home in France
Buying a Home in Italy
Buying a Home in Portugal
Buying a Home in Spain
C++
Calculus
Calligraphy
Cantonese
Car Buying and Maintenance
Card Games
Catalan
Chess
Chi Kung
Chinese Medicine
Christianity
Classical Music
Coaching
Cold War, The
Collecting
Computing for the Over 50s
Consulting
Copywriting
Correct English
Counselling
Creative Writing
Cricket
Croatian
Crystal Healing
CVs
Czech
Danish
Decluttering
Desktop Publishing
Detox

Digital Home Movie Making
Digital Photography
Dog Training
Drawing
Dream Interpretation
Dutch
Dutch Conversation
Dutch Dictionary
Dutch Grammar
Eastern Philosophy
Electronics
English as a Foreign Language
English for International
  Business
English Grammar
English Grammar as a Foreign
  Language
English Vocabulary
Entrepreneurship
Estonian
Ethics
Excel 2003
Feng Shui
Film Making
Film Studies
Finance for Non-Financial
  Managers
Finnish
First World War, The
Fitness
Flash 8
Flash MX
Flexible Working
Flirting
Flower Arranging
Franchising
French
French Conversation
French Dictionary
French Grammar
French Phrasebook
French Starter Kit
French Verbs
French Vocabulary
Freud
Gaelic

Gardening
Genetics
Geology
German
German Conversation
German Grammar
German Phrasebook
German Verbs
German Vocabulary
Globalization
Go
Golf
Good Study Skills
Great Sex
Greek
Greek Conversation
Greek Phrasebook
Growing Your Business
Guitar
Gulf Arabic
Hand Reflexology
Hausa
Herbal Medicine
Hieroglyphics
Hindi
Hindi Conversation
Hinduism
History of Ireland, The
Home PC Maintenance and
  Networking
How to DJ
How to Run a Marathon
How to Win at Casino Games
How to Win at Horse Racing
How to Win at Online Gambling
How to Win at Poker
How to Write a Blockbuster
Human Anatomy & Physiology
Hungarian
Icelandic
Improve Your French
Improve Your German
Improve Your Italian
Improve Your Spanish
Improving Your Employability
Indian Head Massage

Indonesian
Instant French
Instant German
Instant Greek
Instant Italian
Instant Japanese
Instant Portuguese
Instant Russian
Instant Spanish
Internet, The
Irish
Irish Conversation
Irish Grammar
Islam
Italian
Italian Conversation
Italian Grammar
Italian Phrasebook
Italian Starter Kit
Italian Verbs
Italian Vocabulary
Japanese
Japanese Conversation
Java
JavaScript
Jazz
Jewellery Making
Judaism
Jung
Kama Sutra, The
Keeping Aquarium Fish
Keeping Pigs
Keeping Poultry
Keeping a Rabbit
Knitting
Korean
Latin
Latin American Spanish
Latin Dictionary
Latin Grammar
Latvian
Letter Writing Skills
Life at 50: For Men
Life at 50: For Women
Life Coaching
Linguistics

LINUX
Lithuanian
Magic
Mahjong
Malay
Managing Stress
Managing Your Own Career
Mandarin Chinese
Mandarin Chinese Conversation
Marketing
Marx
Massage
Mathematics
Meditation
Middle East Since 1945, The
Modern China
Modern Hebrew
Modern Persian
Mosaics
Music Theory
Mussolini's Italy
Nazi Germany
Negotiating
Nepali
New Testament Greek
NLP
Norwegian
Norwegian Conversation
Old English
One-Day French
One-Day French – the DVD
One-Day German
One-Day Greek
One-Day Italian
One-Day Portuguese
One-Day Spanish
One-Day Spanish – the DVD
Origami
Owning a Cat
Owning a Horse
Panjabi
PC Networking for Small
  Businesses
Personal Safety and Self
  Defence
Philosophy

Philosophy of Mind
Philosophy of Religion
Photography
Photoshop
PHP with MySQL
Physics
Piano
Pilates
Planning Your Wedding
Polish
Polish Conversation
Politics
Portuguese
Portuguese Conversation
Portuguese Grammar
Portuguese Phrasebook
Postmodernism
Pottery
PowerPoint 2003
PR
Project Management
Psychology
Quick Fix French Grammar
Quick Fix German Grammar
Quick Fix Italian Grammar
Quick Fix Spanish Grammar
Quick Fix: Access 2002
Quick Fix: Excel 2000
Quick Fix: Excel 2002
Quick Fix: HTML
Quick Fix: Windows XP
Quick Fix: Word
Quilting
Recruitment
Reflexology
Reiki
Relaxation
Retaining Staff
Romanian
Running Your Own Business
Russian
Russian Conversation
Russian Grammar
Sage Line 50
Sanskrit
Screenwriting

Second World War, The
Serbian
Setting Up a Small Business
Shorthand Pitman 2000
Sikhism
Singing
Slovene
Small Business Accounting
Small Business Health Check
Songwriting
Spanish
Spanish Conversation
Spanish Dictionary
Spanish Grammar
Spanish Phrasebook
Spanish Starter Kit
Spanish Verbs
Spanish Vocabulary
Speaking On Special Occasions
Speed Reading
Stalin's Russia
Stand Up Comedy
Statistics
Stop Smoking
Sudoku
Swahili
Swahili Dictionary
Swedish
Swedish Conversation
Tagalog
Tai Chi
Tantric Sex
Tap Dancing
Teaching English as a Foreign Language
Teams & Team Working
Thai
Theatre
Time Management
Tracing Your Family History
Training
Travel Writing
Trigonometry
Turkish
Turkish Conversation

Twentieth Century USA
Typing
Ukrainian
Understanding Tax for Small Businesses
Understanding Terrorism
Urdu
Vietnamese
Visual Basic
Volcanoes
Watercolour Painting
Weight Control through Diet & Exercise
Welsh
Welsh Dictionary
Welsh Grammar
Wills & Probate
Windows XP
Wine Tasting
Winning at Job Interviews
Word 2003
World Cultures: China
World Cultures: England
World Cultures: Germany
World Cultures: Italy
World Cultures: Japan
World Cultures: Portugal
World Cultures: Russia
World Cultures: Spain
World Cultures: Wales
World Faiths
Writing Crime Fiction
Writing for Children
Writing for Magazines
Writing a Novel
Writing Poetry
Xhosa
Yiddish
Yoga
Zen
Zulu